A GUIDE TO

THE COMEDY OF ERRORS

The Shakespeare Handbooks

Guides available now:

- Antony & Cleopatra
- As You Like It
- The Comedy of Errors
- Hamlet
- Henry IV, Part 1
- Julius Caesar
- King Lear
- Macbeth
- Measure for Measure
- The Merchant of Venice
- A Midsummer Night's Dream
- Othello
- Romeo & Juliet
- The Tempest
- Twelfth Night
- The Winter's Tale

Further titles in preparation.

The Shakespeare Handbooks

A Guide to
The Comedy of Errors

by Alistair McCallum

Upstart Crow Publications

First published in 2020 by
Upstart Crow Publications

Copyright © Alistair McCallum 2020

All rights reserved

A CIP catalogue record for this book is available from the British Library

ISBN 978 1 899747 16 0

Printed in Great Britain by Print2Demand Ltd, 1 Newlands Road, Westoning, Bedfordshire MK45 5LD

www.shakespeare-handbooks.com

Setting the scene

Shakespeare wrote *The Comedy of Errors* in or around 1594, when he was about thirty years old. He had arrived in the London theatre world relatively recently, probably in the late 1580s, as a novice actor; however, while continuing to play smaller roles, he soon turned to writing, and quickly made his mark as a dramatist. His fame was such that, in 1592, a fellow playwright scathingly described the provincial newcomer, who lacked a university education, as 'an upstart crow, beautified with our feathers'.

The Comedy of Errors is fast-paced and tightly constructed; it is Shakespeare's shortest play, and the action takes place in the course of a single frantic afternoon. It seems to have been an immediate success, and the phrase 'a comedy of errors' soon became proverbial for any series of mistakes and misunderstandings.

Over the years, however, the play fell out of favour. Many critics considered the plot – which involves two sets of identical twins – too farcical and lightweight to merit serious attention. Numerous adaptations were created, in which the play was variously rewritten, reordered, abridged, and set to music, but the original play was not performed again for over two hundred years after the author's death.

It was not until the twentieth century that the play was recognised as a brilliant, complex comedy, the work of an accomplished playwright who, even at the start of his career, had adapted material from classical and biblical origins and given it his own distinctive stamp:

"The Comedy of Errors *is an exceptionally skilful composition, wrought from a variety of dramatic and nondramatic sources, judiciously selected and blended ... The radical mix of romance, farce and domestic comedy into such a coherent whole is unique not only among Shakespeare's works, but in the dramatic literature of his age."*

    Charles Whitworth, Introduction to the Oxford Shakespeare edition of *The Comedy of Errors*, 2002

An enigma

A stranger has arrived in the city of Ephesus. Coming originally from Syracuse, hundreds of miles away, he has been travelling for many years.

The visitor has only been in Ephesus for a short time, but now finds himself in grave danger; indeed, he faces a possible death sentence. As the play begins, the man is being questioned sternly by the Duke of Ephesus, who makes it clear that he has no intention of showing leniency.

The captive, however, seems strangely resigned to his fate. Who is this man, and what is his crime? What, or who, has he been searching for on his long, thankless voyage? And why is he so ready to accept the duke's fatal verdict?

Curtain up

An unwelcome stranger I, i

Egeon, a merchant from Syracuse, is in serious trouble. He has been arrested in the city of Ephesus, far from his homeland, and brought before the authorities.

Solinus, the Duke of Ephesus, is addressing the captive solemnly, and is about to hand down his sentence. Egeon, however, seems unafraid. If he suffers the ultimate punishment, he says, it will bring his worries to an end:

> *Egeon:* Proceed, Solinus, to procure my fall,[1]
> And by the doom[2] of death end woes and all.
>
> [1] *bring about my downfall*
> [2] *sentence, penalty*

Egeon's crime, it emerges, is simply that he, a Syracusan, has set foot in Ephesus. Following the recent execution of a number of innocent Ephesian merchants in Syracuse, the duke tells him, relations between the two cities have become extremely hostile. The duke is not disposed to show any mercy:

> *Duke:* ... I am not partial to infringe[1] our laws.
> The enmity and discord which of late
> Sprang from the rancorous outrage of your duke
> To merchants, our well-dealing countrymen,[2]
> Who, wanting guilders to redeem their lives,
> Have sealed his rigorous statutes with their bloods,[3]
> Excludes all pity from our threatening looks ...
>
> [1] *I am not inclined to go against*
> [2] *the malicious cruelty shown by the Duke of Syracuse towards honest traders from Ephesus*
> [3] *who, lacking the money to pay their ransom, have lost their lives under the duke's merciless laws*

Trade between the two cities has been banned; even visiting the opposing city is punishable with a substantial fine. It is clear that Egeon does not have the means to pay, but he seems unconcerned when the duke spells out the consequences:

Duke: ... if any Syracusan born
Come to the Bay of Ephesus, he dies,
His goods confiscate to the Duke's dispose,[1]
Unless a thousand marks be levied
To quit[2] the penalty and ransom him.
Thy substance,[3] valued at the highest rate,
Cannot amount unto a hundred marks:
Therefore, by law thou art condemned to die.
Egeon: Yet this my comfort: when your words are done,
My woes end likewise with the evening sun.

[1] *surrendered to the duke to use as he wishes*
[2] *cancel*
[3] *wealth, assets*

The duke now gives Egeon a chance to explain himself: why, despite the prohibition, has he risked his life by coming to Ephesus?

Shakespeare wrote *The Comedy of Errors* at an early stage in his career as a playwright. However, although the play's basic plot was taken from a Roman comedy, familiar to most of the audience of his time, he was already adapting his source material in radical ways, mingling comic and tragic forms:

"*These scarcely are the accents of comedy, let alone the knockabout farce soon to engulf us. But Shakespeare, who was to become the subtlest of all dramatists, already is very ambiguous in* The Comedy of Errors.*"*

Harold Bloom, *Shakespeare: The Invention of the Human*, 1998

A tale of woe

Egeon, weighed down with grief, can hardly bring himself to describe his circumstances. Nevertheless, he is determined to make it clear that the unhappy state he is now in was brought about by events beyond his control.

He confirms that he is from Syracuse, and married to a Syracusan woman. Their marriage was very happy: they were a prosperous couple, too, thanks to his regular trading voyages to the city of Epidamium. One day, however, his representative in Epidamium died, and Egeon had to travel to the city urgently to attend to his unguarded merchandise.

Some months later, Egeon's wife, heavily pregnant, came to join him in the foreign city. Soon afterwards, she gave birth to identical twin boys; and, by a bizarre coincidence, the same thing happened to another woman staying at the same lodgings. As she was a poor woman, Egeon offered to adopt her boys as servants to his own sons:

Egeon: That very hour, and in the self-same inn,
A meaner [1] woman was delivered
Of such a burden,[2] male twins, both alike.
Those, for [3] their parents were exceeding poor,
I bought, and brought up to attend my sons.

[1] *lowlier, poorer*
[2] *also gave birth to two children*
[3] *since*

Before long, at his wife's request, Egeon agreed to sail back to Syracuse with her and the four children, even though he was anxious about the voyage. His fears were realised when a storm arose soon after they had left Epidamium. As the sky darkened and the wind strengthened, the passengers grew more and more terrified. Finding that the crew had abandoned ship, Egeon and his wife, in desperation, tied themselves and their children to a long wooden beam. As the ship broke up in the storm, the beam floated away on the current with its precious cargo.

Finally the storm subsided and Egeon, to his relief, sighted two ships in the distance heading their way. However, his joy was short-lived. He cannot bring himself to say what happened next, but the duke urges him to continue. He is not unsympathetic to the merchant's plight:

Egeon:	... ere they came – O, let me say no more! Gather the sequel by that went before.[1]
Duke:	Nay, forward, old man; do not break off so, For we may pity, though not pardon thee.
Egeon:	O, had the gods done so, I had not now Worthily termed them merciless to us[2] ...

[1] *as you can imagine, what happened next was as disastrous as what had come before*
[2] *if only the gods had pitied us, I would not now be accusing them, justly, of cruelty*

Before their rescuers arrived, the beam carrying Egeon and his family crashed into a huge rock, and was violently split in two. Egeon watched in horror as his wife was swept away, along with one of their sons and one of their adopted boys, all clinging desperately to their piece of timber.

Eventually, both groups were picked up by the approaching ships. However, the two ships were headed for different destinations, and Egeon's rescuers, who were in a much slower vessel, did not attempt to catch up with the other ship, which sailed off into the distance. Eventually Egeon returned to Syracuse, with his one remaining son and one adopted boy. Since that fateful day, more than twenty years ago, Egeon has not seen his wife or the two boys that were with her.

The duke is curious to know what has happened in the intervening years. Egeon explains that as his son grew up he wanted to know more about his missing twin, and at the age of eighteen he set off with his servant, the adopted boy, who was equally keen to find his own lost brother. Both young men, he mentions, have taken the same name as their respective twins, wanting to keep the memory of their missing brothers alive.

Time passed, and Egeon heard no news of his son or the outcome of his voyage. Eventually, alone and bereft, Egeon decided to set out in search of his lost son. He has travelled far and wide, and was on his way back to his homeland of Syracuse when he decided to call at Ephesus:

Egeon: Five summers have I spent in farthest Greece,
Roaming clean through the bounds of Asia,[1]
And coasting homeward came to Ephesus,
Hopeless to find, yet loath to leave unsought
Or that or any place that harbours men.[2]
But here must end the story of my life …

[1] *wandering along the entire coastline of Asia Minor*
[2] *with no hope of finding my son, but unwilling to leave Ephesus or any other inhabited places unexplored*

The duke is adamant: the law must be respected, and Egeon's sentence cannot be changed. Despite this, he feels great compassion towards the unfortunate merchant, and declares that Egeon has the rest of the day to raise the funds necessary to save him from execution. Egeon, weary and despondent, does not expect to avoid his fate:

Duke: … Yet will I favour thee in what I can.
Therefore, merchant, I'll limit thee this day
To seek thy hope by beneficial help.[1]
Try all the friends thou hast in Ephesus;
Beg thou or borrow to make up the sum,
And live. If no, then thou art doomed to die.

Egeon: … Hopeless and helpless doth Egeon wend,[2]
But to procrastinate his lifeless end.[3]

[1] *I'll allow you the rest of this day to find the ransom money with help from other people*
[2] *set out, wander*
[3] *merely to postpone his inevitable death*

A strange coincidence   I, ii

In a street in Ephesus, two merchants are talking. One of them, a young man from Syracuse named Antipholus, has just arrived. His companion tells him that he must not mention his home city; earlier today, he warns, a merchant from Syracuse was sentenced to death, and will be executed this evening if he cannot pay his ransom.

The local merchant has been safeguarding a purse full of money belonging to Antipholus. He now returns it to the Syracusan, who in turn hands it to his servant Dromio, instructing him to take it to the Centaur, the inn where they are staying while in Ephesus.

Dromio hurries off to the Centaur. It is midday, and Antipholus asks his friend if he wishes to come to the inn for lunch. The merchant has another appointment, but promises to meet Antipholus in the marketplace later in the afternoon.

Antipholus tells his companion that he intends to do some sightseeing in Ephesus before lunch. However, when the merchant leaves it emerges that Antipholus has a different reason for wishing to explore the city:

> *Antipholus of Syracuse:*   I will go lose myself,
> And wander up and down to view the city.
> *Merchant:* Sir, I commend you to your own content.[1] [*Exit.*]
> *Antipholus of Syracuse:* He that commends me to mine own content
> Commends me to the thing I cannot get:
> I to the world am like a drop of water
> That in the ocean seeks another drop;
> Who, failing there to find his fellow forth,
> Unseen, inquisitive, confounds himself.[2]
> So[3] I, to find a mother and a brother,
> In quest of them, unhappy, lose myself.

[1] *I will leave you to do as you please*
[2] *who, failing to find what he is looking for, disappears in confusion, his quest unfulfilled*
[3] *in the same way*

11

> The Ephesus of the play was a Greek city-state in Asia Minor (now Turkey), a trading port famous for its wealth. It was the site of the magnificent Temple of Artemis, one of the Seven Wonders of the Ancient World.
>
> Shakespeare's audience would have been familiar with the name, and would have associated it with paganism and witchcraft: several passages in the Bible describe Saint Paul's encounters with sorcerers and exorcists there, as well as traders selling images of the goddess Artemis. This mixture of money, business, sorcery and trickery pervades the atmosphere of *The Comedy of Errors*.

It now becomes clear: Antipholus is none other than Egeon's son, who left Syracuse many years ago, at the age of eighteen, in search of his twin brother and his mother.

Like Egeon, he is longing to find the rest of his family, from whom he was separated in the cruel shipwreck when he was still a baby: and his search has brought him, like Egeon, to Ephesus.

The plot thickens

Antipholus's servant Dromio, who lost his twin brother in the same shipwreck, was born on the same day as Antipholus. Seeing him often reminds Antipholus of the circumstances of his own birth. He is surprised to see Dromio return now, despite his instruction to wait at the Centaur and guard the money entrusted to him:

> *Antipholus of Syracuse:* Here comes the almanac of my true date.[1]
> – What now? How chance thou art returned so soon?
>
> [1] *the man who, like a calendar, reveals my age and date of birth*

Dromio is baffled by the question. Instead of answering, he scolds his master for his lateness; lunch is ready and waiting.

The lady of the house is in a terrible temper, and she has taken her anger out on her servant:

Dromio of Ephesus: ... The clock hath strucken twelve upon the bell;
My mistress made it one[1] upon my cheek.
She is so hot because the meat is cold;
The meat is cold because you come not home ...

[1] *has struck me once*

Antipholus is equally baffled. He is in no mood for Dromio's eccentric prattling, and demands to know why he has abandoned his master's precious purse at the Centaur:

Antipholus of Syracuse: I am not in a sportive[1] humour now;
Tell me, and dally not:[2] where is the money?
We being strangers here, how dar'st thou trust
So great a charge from thine own custody?[3]

[1] *playful, light-hearted*
[2] *don't waste time*
[3] *how dare you leave such a large sum of money unguarded?*

Dromio repeats his request: his master is late for lunch, and everyone in his household is waiting impatiently for his return. Antipholus, who has only just arrived in Ephesus, is irritated by his servant's nonsensical claims:

Antipholus of Syracuse: Come, Dromio, come, these jests are out of season;
Reserve them till a merrier hour than this.
Where is the gold I gave in charge to thee?
Dromio of Ephesus: To me, sir? Why, you gave no gold to me!
Antipholus of Syracuse: Come on, sir knave, have done your foolishness,
And tell me how thou hast disposed thy charge.[1]
Dromio of Ephesus: My charge was but to fetch you from the mart[2]
Home to your house, the Phoenix, sir, to dinner;
My mistress and her sister stays for you.

[1] *carried out your task (of storing my money safely)*
[2] *marketplace*

> There are plenty of gratuitous beatings in *The Comedy of Errors*. One critic suggests that Shakespeare – possibly against his will – included an element of knockabout, slapstick violence in his early plays to satisfy the demands of his audience:
>
> *"When the first regular theatres were built, they were used not only for the playing of interludes, but for all those activities which had previously been displayed either on raised scaffolds or within improvised spaces in the fields. The citizens delighted in exhibitions of juggling, tumbling, fencing, and wrestling; and these were also provided by the drama. Shakespeare is profuse in his concessions to the athletic interest ...* The Comedy of Errors *is noisy with beatings and the outcries of the victims. All these things were imposed upon Shakespeare by the tastes and habits of his patrons, and by the fashions of the primitive theatre. It was on this robust stock that his towering thought and his delicate fancy were grafted."*
>
> Walter Raleigh, *Shakespeare*, 1957

Eventually, Antipholus strikes his servant in frustration, and Dromio runs off in fright. There can only be one explanation for Dromio's bizarre behaviour, Antipholus believes. The rumours that he has heard about Ephesus must be true:

Antipholus of Syracuse: Upon my life, by some device[1] or other
The villain is o'er-raught of all my money.[2]
They say this town is full of cozenage[3] –
As,[4] nimble jugglers that deceive the eye,
Dark-working sorcerers that change the mind,
Soul-killing witches that deform the body ...

[1] *trick, scheme*
[2] *someone has outwitted my servant, and fooled him into handing over all my gold*
[3] *deception, fraud*
[4] *such as*

Concerned for the security of his money, Antipholus hurries off to the Centaur.

Two views of marriage   II, i

The truth has not dawned on Antipholus. Unbeknown to him, his long-lost twin has settled here in Ephesus, along with his servant. The two men are named Antipholus and Dromio; it was from them, in fact, that the two Syracusans took their names, in honour of their missing brothers.

The puzzling encounter that Antipholus has just had was not with his own servant but with his identical twin, Dromio of Ephesus. This Dromio is now on his way back home, to the Phoenix, where the lady of the house, Adriana, is growing increasingly impatient; it is now two o'clock. She is discussing her husband's lack of punctuality with her sister Luciana.

Luciana takes a more tolerant view of her brother-in-law's negligence. Perhaps he has gone to lunch with one of his fellow merchants, she suggests. Men tend to come and go as they please:

Luciana: Good sister, let us dine, and never fret.
A man is master of his liberty;
Time is their master, and when they see time [1]
They'll go or come: if so, be patient, sister.

[1] *when they feel the time is right*

Adriana is irritated by her sister's attitude. It is not right that one person in a marriage should be controlled by the other, she feels. Luciana insists that failure to conform to her husband's wishes will only lead to discontent:

Adriana: Why should their liberty than ours be more?
Luciana: Because their business still lies out o'door.[1]
Adriana: Look when I serve him so, he takes it ill.[2]
Luciana: O, know[3] he is the bridle of your will.
Adriana: There's none but asses will be bridled so.
Luciana: Why, headstrong liberty is lashed with woe.[4]

[1] *their business always takes them out and about*
[2] *when I act as I please, he takes offence*
[3] *you must be aware*
[4] *wilful disobedience results in unhappiness*

The dominance of males is part of the natural order of things, Luciana believes. Adriana argues that her sister's subservient attitude has prevented her from finding a husband. On the contrary, retorts Luciana, it is the discord that is evident in Adriana's marriage to Antipholus that has put her off. If Luciana were married, she would accept everything, she claims, even infidelity:

Adriana: This servitude makes you to keep unwed.
Luciana: Not this, but troubles of the marriage bed.
Adriana: But were you wedded, you would bear some sway.[1]
Luciana: Ere[2] I learn love, I'll practise to obey.
Adriana: How if your husband start some otherwhere?[3]
Luciana: Till he come home again, I would forbear.[4]

[1] *wield some influence*
[2] *before*
[3] *runs off in a different direction; is unfaithful*
[4] *remain calm and patient*

Saint Paul's letter to the Church at Ephesus, one of the best known books of the New Testament, would certainly have been familiar to an audience of Shakespeare's day. It covered, among other subjects, the nature of domestic relationships.

Luciana's attitude reflects Saint Paul's teachings, but the scene as a whole paints a more nuanced picture:

"It was in his Letter to the Ephesians that Paul exhorted children to obey their parents, servants their masters, and wives their husbands. The action of the play seems to call these demands into question: how can you obey your parents when they are lost, or your master when he gives you contradictory orders? And should a woman obey her husband when he is unworthy of her?"

Jonathan Bate, Introduction to the RSC Shakespeare edition of *The Comedy of Errors*, 2011

Adriana is scornful of her sister's naïve view of marriage. It is easy for her to talk of obedience and acceptance: if she marries, and finds herself troubled by her husband's unreliability, she will no doubt take a different view. One day, replies Luciana, she may give marriage a try, just to find out.

A heartfelt complaint

Dromio now returns to the Phoenix. Adriana demands to know why he has not brought her husband back with him, but his answers are ambiguous. He found Antipholus in the marketplace as instructed, but the encounter was confusing and painful:

Adriana: ... is your tardy[1] master now at hand?[2]
Dromio of Ephesus: Nay, he's at two hands with me, and that my two ears can witness.
Adriana: Say, didst thou speak with him? Knowst thou his mind?
Dromio of Ephesus: Ay, ay, he told his mind upon mine ear; Beshrew his hand, I scarce could understand it.[3]

[1] *late, unpunctual*
[2] *nearby, approaching*
[3] *he made his feelings clear when he slapped my ears, but I still didn't know what he meant*

All that his master wanted to talk about was his gold, reports Dromio: he was not interested in his lunch, his wife or his house. Adriana orders Dromio to stop his foolery and go back to the marketplace to fetch Antipholus.

Dromio, fearful of another beating from Antipholus, begs Adriana to send some other messenger: however, the result is another beating, this time from the exasperated Adriana, and Dromio runs away indignantly.

Luciana cannot help noticing that her sister is in a particularly troubled frame of mind. The reason for Adriana's distress at her husband's lateness now becomes clear: she confesses that she suspects him of spending time with other women. She feels unloved, and believes that the lack of attention from her husband has made her duller and less attractive:

Adriana: His company must do his minions grace,[1]
Whilst I at home starve for a merry look.
Hath homely age th'alluring beauty took
From my poor cheek? Then he hath wasted it.
Are my discourses[2] dull? Barren my wit?
If voluble and sharp discourse be marred,
Unkindness blunts it more than marble hard.[3]

[1] *he lavishes his attention on his darlings*
[2] *conversations*
[3] *if my conversation is no longer fluent and quick-witted, it's because it has been blunted by his negligence*

Even her clothes, she complains, are not as eye-catching as those of her rivals; this too is her husband's fault, as he is in charge of their money. Above all, she wishes that he would be more considerate and loving towards her. Luciana rebukes her sister for her unfounded jealousy:

Adriana: My decayed fair[1]
A sunny look of his would soon repair.
But, too-unruly deer, he breaks the pale[2]
And feeds from home;[3] poor I am but his stale.[4]
Luciana: Self-harming jealousy! Fie, beat it hence.

[1] *my fading beauty*
[2] *fence, enclosure*
[3] *gratifies his desires away from home*
[4] *to him, I am nothing more than a worthless, worn-out mistress*

Adriana mentions that her husband has promised her a necklace. She would gladly do without it, she tells her sister, if Antipholus would instead treat her with more consideration.

> *His company must do his minions grace ...*
>
> At some point in the 1580s, William Shakespeare took the momentous decision to leave Stratford-upon-Avon and pursue a career in the rapidly growing but precarious world of London theatre. He was in his twenties, and already married with three children. He was living, with his new family, in his father John's house. In all probability he was providing much-needed help in his father's glove-making workshop; John Shakespeare's shady business dealings had by now brought him to the verge of bankruptcy.
>
> One critic has speculated that Adriana's complaints may echo the sentiments that Shakespeare's wife, Anne Hathaway, would have expressed at her husband's reckless decision:
>
> *"Here was the eldest son and potential prop of the family of John Shakespeare, here a husband and father of three, abandoning his home, his work, his livelihood ... It is difficult to imagine Mistress Anne taking this resolve calmly. There would be little or no help from her now financially embarrassed father-in-law ... If Anne had a tongue, she had cause to use it now, when she saw him risking everything for a caprice or an ambition that seemed to her idle and absurd ... Some of his wife's bitterness against the new 'minions' who had lured him away to London may be heard, perhaps, in Adriana's cry."*
>
> Ivor Brown, *Shakespeare*, 1949

Another innocent victim II, ii

Back in the marketplace, Antipholus of Syracuse is feeling relieved: he has been to the Centaur and found that his gold is safe and sound. He is puzzled, however, by his recent conversation with Dromio. How did his servant manage to take his purse back to the inn and reappear in front of him so quickly? Ephesus is a bewildering place.

Dromio now appears, and Antipholus questions him closely about his earlier antics, when he pretended to know nothing about the gold or the inn, and said various incomprehensible things about coming home to have lunch with his wife. If he has not come to his senses, Antipholus warns, he is likely to suffer another beating:

Antipholus of Syracuse: How now, sir, is your merry humour altered?
As you love strokes, so jest with me again.[1]
You know no Centaur? You received no gold?
Your mistress sent to have me home to dinner?
My house was at the Phoenix? Wast thou mad,
That thus so madly thou didst answer me?

[1] *if you love being beaten, carry on with your prank*

It is now Dromio's turn to be baffled. For this is not Dromio of Ephesus, servant to Adriana and her husband: this is Dromio of Syracuse, who has dutifully stored his master's gold at the Centaur inn as instructed. He knows nothing of the presence of his identical twin in Ephesus, nor of the conversation that his master has just had with the other Dromio.

Dromio assumes that his master is playing some kind of practical joke. This infuriates Antipholus even further, and in frustration he beats his innocent servant:

Dromio of Syracuse: I did not see you since you sent me hence,[1]
Home to the Centaur with the gold you gave me.
Antipholus of Syracuse: Villain, thou didst deny the gold's receipt,
And told'st me of a mistress and a dinner,
For which I hope thou felt'st I was displeased.[2]
Dromio of Syracuse: I am glad to see you in this merry vein;
What means this jest? I pray you, master, tell me.
Antipholus of Syracuse: Yea, dost thou jeer and flout me in the teeth?[3]
Think'st thou I jest? Hold, take thou that, and that!
[*Beats Dromio.*]

[1] *away from here*
[2] *I hope the fact that I beat you made you realise how annoyed I was*
[3] *mock me to my face*

There is a time and place for childish tricks, says Antipholus. If Dromio tries to play the fool when his master is in a serious mood, he is likely to suffer for it. Dromio is none the wiser; after all, he has not been playing the fool. Antipholus, calming down, flippantly suggests that he might stop paying his servant:

Dromio of Syracuse: Was there ever any man thus beaten out of season,[1]
 When in the why and the wherefore is neither rhyme nor reason?
 Well, sir, I thank you.
Antipholus of Syracuse: Thank me, sir, for what?
Dromio of Syracuse: Marry, sir, for this something that you gave me for nothing.
Antipholus of Syracuse: I'll make you amends next, to give you nothing for something.[2]

[1] *at the wrong time*
[2] *to pay you nothing for your services*

Now reconciled, the two men relax and engage in a mock argument. There is a time for everything, claims Antipholus again. Dromio disagrees: there is no time for a bald man to recover his hair, for example. Time allows beasts to grow plenty of hair, Dromio points out, but is not so generous to men, endowing them instead with intelligence.

Antipholus counters that there are many dim-witted men with full heads of hair. All such men are clever enough to lose their hair, retorts Dromio, however dim they may be:

Dromio of Syracuse: ... what he hath scanted[1] men in hair he hath given them in wit.
Antipholus of Syracuse: Why, but there's many a man hath more hair than wit.
Dromio of Syracuse: Not a man of those but he hath the wit to lose his hair.[2]

[1] *provided inadequately, been ungenerous*
[2] *every one of them knows how to lose his hair by catching syphilis*

The men's amiable banter is interrupted as a woman comes to the marketplace, waving to Antipholus. He has no idea who she is, but she is clearly determined to get his attention.

The wrong Antipholus

Adriana, having come to the marketplace in search of her husband, is dismayed to find her worst fears confirmed. Antipholus seems to have lost interest in her completely, and is treating her more like a stranger than a wife. She remembers wistfully how different things used to be, and how much her husband has changed:

Adriana: Ay, ay, Antipholus, look strange and frown:
Some other mistress hath thy sweet aspects;[1]
I am not Adriana, nor thy wife.
The time was once when thou unurged[2] wouldst vow
That never words were music to thine ear,
That never object pleasing in thine eye,
That never touch well welcome to thy hand,
That never meat sweet-savoured in thy taste,
Unless I spake, or looked, or touched, or carved to thee.
How comes it now, my husband, O, how comes it,
That thou art then estranged from thyself?

[1] *your loving looks*
[2] *spontaneously, without prompting*

When she reaches out towards Antipholus, he pulls away in alarm. Whatever he does, she responds, the two of them can never be separated:

Adriana: ... as easy mayst thou fall
A drop of water in the breaking gulf,[1]
And take unmingled thence that drop again[2]
Without addition or diminishing,
As take from me thyself, and not me too.

[1] *it would be as easy to allow a drop of water to fall into the crashing waves*
[2] *retrieve it exactly as it was*

Antipholus would be angry and wounded, says Adriana, if he were to discover that she was unfaithful, and it is the same for her. Their well-being, and the integrity of their marriage, depend on fidelity and mutual trust:

Adriana: ... if we two be one, and thou play false,
I do digest the poison of thy flesh,
Being strumpeted by thy contagion.[1]
Keep, then, fair league and truce with thy true bed[2] ...

[1] *being contaminated and turned into a whore by your adultery*
[2] *keep your vow, and stay faithful to your rightful marriage-bed*

Antipholus, who has been listening carefully, responds to the lady as tactfully as he can. He informs her, politely, that he has no idea who she is or what she is talking about:

Antipholus of Syracuse: Plead you to me, fair dame? I know you not:
In Ephesus I am but two hours old,[1]
As strange unto your town as to your talk,[2]
Who, every word by all my wit being scanned,
Wants wit in all, one word to understand.[3]

[1] *I have only been in this town for two hours*
[2] *what you say is strange to me, just as your town is unfamiliar*
[3] *I've puzzled over your speech with all my wits, but despite my best efforts I can't understand a word of it*

Plead you to me, fair dame?

"*As so often, Shakespeare has it both ways: this is at one and the same time the moving testimony of a neglected wife responding to her husband's sexual infidelity and the cue for the line that invariably wins the play's biggest laugh ... she is, of course, confronting the wrong brother."*

Jonathan Bate, Introduction to the RSC Shakespeare edition of *The Comedy of Errors*, 2011

Adriana has her way

On hearing Antipholus's denial, Luciana is offended on her sister's behalf. To Dromio's alarm, she names him as the messenger who was sent to fetch Antipholus. Adriana reminds the servant that he came back bruised and bewildered by the encounter:

Luciana: Fie, brother![1] How the world is changed with you:
When were you wont to use my sister thus?
She sent for you by Dromio home to dinner.
Antipholus of Syracuse: By Dromio?
Dromio of Syracuse: By me?
Adriana: By thee, and this thou didst return from him:[2]
That he did buffet thee, and, in his blows,
Denied my house for his, me for his wife.[3]

[1] *brother-in-law*
[2] *this is what you reported when you came back*
[3] *he beat you, denying that he knew anything about me or our house*

Antipholus turns angrily to Dromio. When his servant first returned from the Centaur, he recalls, Dromio babbled on about his master's wife and house in Ephesus, and Antipholus beat him as punishment for talking nonsense. Although Dromio continues to plead his innocence, Antipholus suspects that he is in league with these two strangers, though his motive is not clear. The fact that they know his name alarms him: if Dromio has never met them, how could they have found out? Anything is possible, it seems, in this strange city.

Adriana, meanwhile, has made up her mind to remain calm and to concentrate on strengthening her relationship with her husband. He has undoubtedly mistreated her, and is clearly engaged in some foolish pretence involving their servant, but she is determined to rise above the situation. She takes his arm:

Adriana: How ill agrees it with your gravity[1]
To counterfeit thus grossly with your slave,
Abetting him to thwart me in my mood.[2]
… Come, I will fasten on this sleeve of thine:

Thou art an elm, my husband, I a vine,
Whose weakness, married to thy stronger state,
Makes me with thy strength to communicate.³
If aught possess thee from me, it is dross⁴ ...

¹ *it doesn't suit your serious nature*
² *to collude with your slave in this clumsy attempt to upset me*
³ *enables me to share your strength*
⁴ *anything that tries to take you away from me is worthless, and must be removed*

Antipholus is taken aback by the stranger's boldness. He is still utterly mystified, but decides to go along with events to see what happens:

Antipholus of Syracuse: [*aside*] ... was I married to her in my dream?
Or sleep I now and think I hear all this?¹
What error drives our eyes and ears amiss?²
Until I know this sure uncertainty,³
I'll entertain the offered fallacy.⁴

¹ *am I asleep now, and imagining all this?*
² *what delusion is causing these strange experiences?*
³ *this definite mystery*
⁴ *I'll treat the deception that has been presented to me as if it were real*

What error drives our eyes and ears amiss?

"The Comedy of Errors *is deeply concerned with questions of identity and selfhood ... the twin Antipholuses and Dromios enter a world of madness when they are repeatedly mistaken for one another. 'Error' here has a stronger connotation than our modern sense of 'mistake'; it is a terrifying condition of spiritual and intellectual wandering (from the Latin verb* errare, *to wander astray).*"

Laurie Maguire and Emma Smith, *30 Great Myths about Shakespeare*, 2013

Dromio too decides to co-operate with the strangers, but in his case it is terror, not curiosity, that motivates him:

Dromio of Syracuse: This is the fairy land; O, spite of spites,
We talk with goblins, owls and sprites!
If we obey them not, this will ensue:
They'll suck our breath[1] or pinch us black and blue.

[1] *suffocate us*

Adriana walks resolutely towards the Phoenix, holding Antipholus firmly by the arm. She resolves to stop agonising about their marriage: instead, she will have a heart-to-heart conversation with her husband about his many misdemeanours, hoping to clear the air and make a fresh start. The two of them are to dine together, in a private upstairs chamber. She orders Dromio to guard the front door and tell any visitors that her husband is not at home: on no account is anyone else to enter the building.

Antipholus allows himself to be led to the lady's house, confused but intrigued by the dreamlike situation. He decides to follow this strange adventure wherever it leads:

Antipholus of Syracuse: Am I in earth, in heaven or in hell?
Sleeping or waking? Mad or well advised?[1]
Known unto these, and to myself disguised?[2]
I'll say as they say, and persever so,[3]
And in this mist at all adventures go.[4]

[1] *rational, in my right mind*
[2] *how is it that these people know me, yet I don't know who I'm supposed to be?*
[3] *I'll agree with everything they say, and stick with my role*
[4] *press ahead through the confusion, however doubtful I feel and whatever the risks*

After its initial success, *The Comedy of Errors* seems to have fallen into neglect; for over two hundred years, it was not staged again in its original form. Critics and scholars long considered it an immature play, full of improbable events, and possibly not even the work of Shakespeare:

"The play is supposed, by some commentators, to have been among Shakespeare's earliest productions; whilst others will not allow that he had any farther share in the work, than to embellish it with additional words, lines, speeches, or scenes, to gratify its original author, or the manager of the theatre. Of all improbable stories, this is the most so ... Its fable[1] verges on impossibility, and the incidents which arise from it could never have occurred."

[1] *plot*

Elizabeth Inchbald, *The British Theatre*, 1808

Latecomers III, i

Adriana's husband Antipholus, completely unaware of the presence of his identical twin in Ephesus, is approaching the Phoenix. He has brought two companions home for lunch: the goldsmith Angelo, who has been working on a necklace ordered by Antipholus for his wife, and the merchant Balthazar.

Antipholus is anxious. He is late for lunch, and is only too aware that his lack of punctuality is a source of irritation to Adriana. The reason for his lateness is the length of time he spent in the goldsmith's shop, and he asks Angelo to back up his excuse:

Antipholus of Ephesus: Good signor Angelo, you must excuse us all;[1]
My wife is shrewish when I keep not hours.[2]
Say that I lingered with you at your shop
To see the making of her carcanet,[3]
And that tomorrow you will bring it home.

[1] *apologise to Adriana on our behalf*
[2] *my wife becomes bad-tempered if I come home late*
[3] *necklace*

His servant Dromio has been behaving very strangely today, Antipholus tells his friends. Earlier, the man claimed that his master had beaten him, made wild accusations about hiding a huge amount of gold, and pretended to know nothing of his own wife and home.

Antipholus has no idea where his servant's strange imaginings have come from, but he suspects drink is involved. Dromio, resentful of the unjustified beating he received from his master, refuses to change his story. He still has the bruises from their earlier encounter:

Antipholus of Ephesus: ... here's a villain that would face me down [1]
He met me on the mart, and that I beat him
And charged him with [2] a thousand marks in gold,
And that I did deny my wife and house.
Thou drunkard, thou, what didst thou mean by this?
Dromio of Ephesus: Say what you will, sir, but I know what I know;
That you beat me at the mart I have your hand [3] to show.
If the skin were parchment and the blows you gave were ink,
Your own handwriting would tell you what I think.

[1] *boldly claim to my face*
[2] *accused him of possessing*
[3] *handprint*

Antipholus turns to Balthazar, who seems subdued. Antipholus hopes that his spirits will be raised by the food and the friendly reception on offer. The latter is more precious, answers Balthazar:

Antipholus of Ephesus: Pray God our cheer [1]
May answer [2] my good will and your good welcome here.
Balthazar: I hold your dainties cheap, sir, and your welcome dear. [3]

[1] *food and drink*
[2] *demonstrate*
[3] *your fine food is of little value compared to the warmth of your welcome*

A brief debate follows. A warm welcome is not enough, insists Antipholus: good food is just as important, if not more so. A welcome, after all, is nothing more than words. Balthazar disagrees, claiming that good fellowship is what matters.

Finally, Antipholus courteously apologises in advance for the quality of his food, but promises that his guests will be received cordially:

Antipholus of Ephesus: … though my cates[1] be mean, take them in
good part:
Better cheer may you have, but not with better heart.[2]

[1] *delicacies, fine dishes*
[2] *you may find better food elsewhere, but not served with more genuine hospitality*

At this point, Antipholus tries to open his front door. To his surprise, it is locked.

Dromio versus Dromio

Dromio calls out to the staff inside the Phoenix to let them in. The only reply, however, is a stream of insults and a blank refusal from the other side of the door. Unaware that he is speaking to his twin brother, Dromio asks angrily who is guarding the door:

Dromio of Syracuse: … Go, get thee from the door.
Dromio of Ephesus: What patch[1] is made our porter? – My master
stays[2] in the street.
Dromio of Syracuse: Let him walk from whence he came, lest he
catch cold on's feet.

[1] *fool*
[2] *is waiting*

Antipholus, indignant at being locked out of his own home, adds his voice to Dromio's. The servant is appalled to learn that there is an impostor inside the house:

Antipholus of Ephesus: ... I have not dined today.
Dromio of Syracuse: Nor today here you must not; come again when you may.
Antipholus of Ephesus: What art thou that keep'st me out from the house I owe?[1]
Dromio of Syracuse: The porter for this time, sir, and my name is Dromio.
Dromio of Ephesus: O villain, thou hast stolen both mine office[2] and my name ...

[1] *own*
[2] *position, job*

A kitchen maid now joins Dromio of Syracuse behind the door, and adds to the commotion, shouting out defiantly to the strangers. Outside, Antipholus and Dromio start banging at the door, threatening to punish the staff who are keeping them out.

At this point, disturbed by all the noise, Adriana appears at a window above the street, and demands to know what is happening. Dromio, guarding the door, tells her that there is a mob of unruly boys outside. Antipholus, outside, calls out to his wife: but she cannot see him from her window, and orders him away angrily.

Antipholus's two companions have been standing aside during the chaotic scene. They remark that, in the circumstances, they are unlikely to get either a meal or a welcome. Their earlier discussion about hospitality seems rather meaningless now:

Angelo: Here is neither cheer, sir, nor welcome; we would fain[1] have either.
Balthazar: In debating which was best, we shall part with neither.

[1] *gladly, gratefully*

Antipholus bears a grudge

Unable to persuade anyone to let him into his house, Antipholus is growing increasingly agitated. Eventually he decides to break in by force, and orders Dromio to find a crowbar.

His friend Balthazar is shocked at the idea. There must be a good reason why his wife has decided to lock the doors, he argues, even though it is a mystery at the moment. Adriana is a woman of good sense and judgement, and any attempt to enter the building forcibly would cast doubt on her reputation. Instead, they should leave quietly and eat at an inn in the city:

> *Balthazar:* ... Her sober virtue, years and modesty
> Plead on her part some cause to you unknown; [1]
> And doubt not, sir, but she will well excuse
> Why at this time the doors are made against you. [2]
> Be ruled by me: [3] depart in patience,
> And let us to the Tiger all to dinner ...
>
> [1] *suggest that there must be a reason for her actions that you are not aware of*
> [2] *you can be sure that she will give a good explanation for the fact that you have been shut out*
> [3] *take my advice*

"The play delights in change: shifts in tone, in genre convention, in poetic or prose form. The effect can even become disconcerting, for poking through the surface of the buffoonery are intimations of sorrow, embarrassment, anxiety and suffered abuse – cries of the heart from the other side of farce."

Kent Cartwright, Introduction to the Arden Shakespeare edition of *The Comedy of Errors*, 2016

Breaking in now, in broad daylight, would lead to gossip and speculation, and Antipholus's reputation might never recover. It would be better, advises Balthazar, for him to come back on his own later in the day.

Antipholus agrees, but he is determined to have his revenge on Adriana. He proposes that the three of them dine at the Porcupine, the house of a courtesan he knows well. Although the woman is a professional escort, he maintains that their relationship is innocent. All the same, he knows that his wife would rather he kept away from her:

> *Antipholus of Ephesus:* I know a wench of excellent discourse,
> Pretty and witty, wild and yet, too, gentle.[1]
> There will we dine. This woman that I mean,
> My wife – but I protest without desert –
> Hath oftentimes upbraided me withal.[2]
>
> [1] *high-spirited but sensitive*
> [2] *my wife has often complained to me about her, although I insist she has no reason to do so*

Antipholus asks the goldsmith Angelo to go back to his workshop to fetch the gold necklace that he has created, and bring it to the Porcupine when they meet later on. The necklace was to be a present for Adriana; just to show how angry he is at being locked out of his house, Antipholus intends to give it to the courtesan instead.

Love at first sight   III, ii

Luciana is talking to Antipholus of Syracuse, the man she believes to be her sister's husband. He has left the company of Adriana, and Luciana is rebuking him for his inconsiderate attitude towards their marriage.

The least he can do, urges Luciana, is to show his wife some compassion, even if he does not love her. If he is having affairs with other women, he should be discreet about it:

Luciana: If you did wed my sister for her wealth,
Then for her wealth's sake use[1] her with more kindness.
Or if you like elsewhere,[2] do it by stealth:
Muffle your false love with some show of blindness;
Let not my sister read it in your eye[3] …

[1] *treat*
[2] *if you stray outside your marriage*
[3] *conceal your love for other women; make sure it doesn't show in your eyes*

Being unfaithful is bad enough, she argues; failing to hide his infidelity is adding insult to injury. She appeals to her brother-in-law to go back to Adriana's chamber and talk to her:

Luciana: 'Tis double wrong to truant with your bed[1]
And let her read it in thy looks at board.[2]
 … gentle brother, get you in again;
Comfort my sister, cheer her, call her 'wife'.

[1] *to visit another woman's bed*
[2] *let her see it in your face at meal times*

Antipholus does not know who this beautiful stranger is, nor how she came to know his name; all he knows is that he has fallen completely under her spell. Addressing her with tenderness and devotion, he asks her to enlighten him. He does not understand why or how she is trying to influence him:

Antipholus of Syracuse: Teach me, dear creature, how to think and speak;
Lay open to my earthy, gross conceit[1] –
Smothered in errors, feeble, shallow, weak –
The folded meaning of your words' deceit.[2]
Against my soul's pure truth why labour you
To make it wander in an unknown field?[3]

[1] *my limited, dull understanding*
[2] *the hidden meaning of your complex words*
[3] *why are you trying to turn me away from what my soul knows to be right?*

33

Antipholus has no interest in the woman who first accosted him: it is Luciana who has captivated him. He implores her to talk not of her sister, but of herself:

Antipholus of Syracuse: ... if that I am I,[1] then well I know,
     Your weeping sister is no wife of mine,
     Nor to her bed no homage do I owe.[2]
     Far more, far more, to you do I decline.[3]
     O, train me not, sweet mermaid, with thy note,
     To drown me in thy sister's flood of tears:[4]
     Sing, siren, for thyself, and I will dote.

[1] *if I am myself*
[2] *I haven't made any promises to her; I'm not obliged to be faithful to her*
[3] *I lean in your direction, I am attracted to you*
[4] *do not lure me, with your sweet singing, into your sister's tearful embrace*

Luciana is horrified. She is aware that Adriana's marriage is not perfect, but is astonished to find her husband blatantly making advances in this way. She tries unsuccessfully to deter him, reminding him of his commitment to his wife.

Eventually Antipholus reaches out to take Luciana's hand, and she runs off in distress. Adriana must be told the truth about her husband, she decides:

Antipholus of Syracuse: Thee will I love, and with thee lead my life;
     Thou hast no husband yet, nor I no wife:
     Give me thy hand.
Luciana: O, soft, sir, hold you still;[1]
     I'll fetch my sister to get her good will.[2]

[1] *stop, restrain yourself*
[2] *to find out what she intends to do about this*

Another romantic entanglement

Just as Luciana leaves, Dromio charges in breathlessly. Like Antipholus, he has almost forgotten who he is in this strange place:

Dromio of Syracuse: Do you know me, sir? Am I Dromio? Am I your man? Am I myself?

Dromio, it emerges, is running from Nell, a kitchen maid at the Phoenix. Nell is married to Dromio of Ephesus, and has clearly not realised that her husband's role in the household has been taken by his identical twin. The new servant is appalled to find that he is spoken for:

Dromio of Syracuse: I am an ass, I am a woman's man, and besides myself.
Antipholus of Syracuse: What woman's man? And how besides thyself?
Dromio of Syracuse: Marry, sir, besides myself I am due to a woman:[1] one that claims me, one that haunts me,[2] one that will have me.
Antipholus of Syracuse: What claim lays she to thee?[3]
Dromio of Syracuse: Marry, sir, such claim as you would lay to your horse[4] ...

[1] *I belong to a woman, not just to myself*
[2] *pursues me relentlessly*
[3] *what right does she claim over you?*
[4] *she owns me, just as you might own a horse*

Dromio finds the woman abhorrent, and he gives an extravagant description of her physical features. Years of working in the kitchen have taken their toll:

Dromio of Syracuse: Marry, sir, she's the kitchen wench, and all grease; and I know not what use to put her to but to make a lamp[1] of her, and run from her by her own light.

[1] *an oil lamp*

The kitchen maid is extremely stout, too, he claims:

Antipholus of Syracuse: Then she bears some breadth?
Dromio of Syracuse: No longer from head to foot than from hip to hip: she is spherical, like a globe. I could find out countries in her.

Antipholus asks, teasingly, where various countries might be on Nell's body. Dromio takes the opportunity to indulge in some crude mockery at the kitchen maid's expense:

Antipholus of Syracuse: In what part of her body stands Ireland?
Dromio of Syracuse: Marry, sir, in her buttocks; I found it out by the bogs.[1]
Antipholus of Syracuse: ... Where England?
Dromio of Syracuse: I looked for the chalky cliffs,[2] but I could find no whiteness in them.
Antipholus of Syracuse: ... Where America, the Indies?
Dromio of Syracuse: O, sir, upon her nose, all o'er embellished with rubies, carbuncles, sapphires[3] ...

[1] *the spongy flesh of her backside*
[2] *her teeth*
[3] *pimples, boils and pustules*

There was a more serious side to his encounter with Nell, reports Dromio. As well as claiming that they were married, she knew his name; what was more, she could prove that she knew him intimately by listing various features hidden under his clothes. He is convinced that witchcraft is involved.

Antipholus finds his servant's revelations unnerving, and he resolves to leave Ephesus as soon as possible. He sends Dromio to the harbour to enquire if any ships are due to leave the city: he is to bring news of any departures to the marketplace, where Antipholus will be waiting. Dromio, only too happy to get away from the terrifying kitchen maid, sprints off to the dockside.

Alone, Antipholus reflects on this perplexing city, where everyone seems to know him and his servant even though they have just arrived for the first time. He is keen to escape from the woman who insists, mystifyingly, that she is his wife. Leaving her sister, on the other hand, will be painful. He must not allow himself to be tempted:

Antipholus of Syracuse: ... her fair sister,
Possessed with such a gentle, sovereign grace,
Of such enchanting presence and discourse,[1]
Hath almost made me traitor to myself.
But lest myself be guilty of self-wrong,
I'll stop mine ears against the mermaid's song.[2]

[1] *speech, conversation*
[2] *I'll refuse to be captivated by this beautiful but dangerous creature*

... I'll stop mine ears against the mermaid's song.

Belief in the existence of mermaids was widespread in Shakespeare's time. In 1608 the English explorer Henry Hudson, while sailing north of Scandinavia, wrote in the ship's log:

"This morning, one of our companie looking over boord saw a mermaid ... shee was come close to the ship's side, looking earnestly on the men ... from the navill upward, her backe and breasts were like a woman's, as they say that saw her; her body as big as one of us; her skin very white; and long haire hanging downe behinde, of colour blacke: in her going downe they saw her tayle, which was like the tayle of a porposse, and speckled like a macrell."

Hudson seemed untroubled by the sighting. However, in the popular imagination, mermaids were associated with the Sirens of Greek mythology, half-human birdlike creatures that sang with irresistible beauty, luring sailors to their deaths on rocky outcrops.

Gold from a stranger

Antipholus's thoughts are interrupted as a visitor approaches. It is the goldsmith Angelo, bringing the necklace ordered by Adriana's husband. He had intended to come to the Porcupine earlier to have lunch with Antipholus and Balthazar, but finishing the chain took longer than expected.

As he hands over the chain, Angelo is amused by his friend's apparent puzzlement:

Antipholus of Syracuse: What is your will that I shall do with this?
Angelo: What please yourself,[1] sir: I have made it for you.
Antipholus of Syracuse: Made it for me, sir? I bespoke it not.[2]
Angelo: Not once, nor twice, but twenty times you have.
Go home with it, and please your wife withal[3] ...

[1] *whatever you wish*
[2] *I did not ask for it*
[3] *with it*

Angelo will return for payment later in the afternoon. Antipholus offers to pay immediately, in case the two of them never meet again. Once more, Angelo finds his friend's feigned ignorance hilarious:

Angelo: ... at supper-time I'll visit you,
And then receive my money for the chain.
Antipholus of Syracuse: I pray you, sir, receive the money now,
For fear you ne'er see chain nor money more.[1]
Angelo: You are a merry man, sir; fare you well.

[1] *in case you never get your money or see your chain again*

Angelo leaves, and Antipholus examines the precious gold chain. It would be absurd not to keep it, he decides, and he slips it around his neck. In this peculiar city, he reflects, wealth is easy to come by:

Antipholus of Syracuse: What I should think of this I cannot tell;
    But this I think: there's no man is so vain [1]
    That would refuse so fair an offered chain.
    I see a man here needs not live by shifts,[2]
    When in the streets he meets such golden gifts.

    [1] *foolish, misguided*
    [2] *stratagems, crafty schemes*

Antipholus now sets off for the marketplace, to see if Dromio has any news of departing ships: the unexpected gift has not changed his mind, and he is determined to get away as soon as possible.

"*We spend our lives partly in a waking world we call normal and partly in a dream world which we create out of our own desires. Shakespeare endows both worlds with equal imaginative power, brings them opposite one another, and makes each world seem unreal when seen by the light of the other.*"

Northrop Frye, *Anatomy of Criticism*, 1957

An unpaid debt
IV, i

In the marketplace, a merchant of Ephesus has come to find Angelo. The goldsmith owes him a large sum of money which the merchant needs urgently, as he is due to leave shortly on a trading mission to Persia. To be absolutely sure of receiving his money, the merchant has engaged the services of an officer of the law, a bailiff who has the power to arrest Angelo if he refuses to pay.

Angelo is untroubled by the sudden demand. He explains amicably that, at this very moment, he is on his way to see Antipholus, a customer who is due to pay him for an expensive gold necklace. He invites the merchant to walk with him to his customer's house. As they set off, however, Antipholus himself appears.

The man they have spotted is Antipholus of Ephesus. He has just left the Porcupine, the courtesan's house where – having been locked out of his own home – he went for lunch. He is still in a vengeful frame of mind, and intends to punish his wife and her accomplices severely. He sends his servant away on an errand:

> *Antipholus of Ephesus:* ... go thou
> And buy a rope's end.[1] That will I bestow
> Among my wife and her confederates[2]
> For locking me out of my doors by day.
>
> [1] *a short, thick piece of rope, used for flogging*
> [2] *I'll use it on my wife and those who helped her*

When Antipholus sees Angelo, he expresses his irritation that the goldsmith did not come to the Porcupine for lunch. He was supposed to bring the necklace, which Antipholus wanted as a present for the courtesan. As it is, she has been left empty-handed.

> The strange, dreamlike atmosphere of Ephesus is reinforced by frequent references to animals, both real and imaginary:
>
> *"The workaday city of Ephesus itself is curiously animate: its buildings and houses bear the names of exotic fauna – Centaur, Phoenix, Tiger and Porcupine. More than thirty names of animals, real and legendary, generic and specific, occur in the play."*
>
> Charles Whitworth, Introduction to the Oxford Shakespeare edition of *The Comedy of Errors*, 2002

Angelo is unsure what to make of his friend's remarks: it was only a short time ago that he saw Antipholus and gave him the chain, explaining that he would be back later for payment. Presumably Antipholus is joking, as he was at their last meeting. However, now that Angelo needs the money immediately in order to pay the merchant – who is standing by with a bailiff – the joke is wearing rather thin. He hands over his invoice:

Angelo: Saving your merry humour,[1] here's the note
How much your chain weighs to the utmost carat,
The fineness of the gold and chargeful fashion,[2]
Which doth amount to three odd ducats more
Than I stand debted to this gentleman.
I pray you see him presently discharged[3] ...

[1] *joking apart; with all due respect for your cheerful banter*
[2] *expensive craftsmanship*
[3] *paid in full immediately*

Antipholus does not have the sum to hand. As he has some other business to conduct in the city, he suggests that Angelo and the merchant go directly to the Phoenix and ask his wife for the money. As long as they show her the chain, she will pay them promptly.

Angelo agrees and, impatient to go, asks Antipholus for the chain. He replies irritably that he does not have it; he assumes the goldsmith has it, as he was due to bring it to their lunchtime gathering. The merchant, for his part, needs the money urgently, as his ship is due to leave shortly. The argument soon builds to an angry, confused crescendo:

Merchant: [*to Angelo*] The hour steals on; I pray you, sir, dispatch.
Angelo: [*to Antipholus*] You hear how he importunes[1] me. – The chain!
Antipholus of Ephesus: Why, give it to my wife, and fetch your money.
Angelo: Come, come, you know I gave it to you even now. Either send the chain, or send me by some token.[2]
Antipholus of Ephesus: Fie! Now you run this humour out of breath.[3] Come, where's the chain? I pray you, let me see it.
Merchant: My business cannot brook this dalliance.[4]

[1] *begs, pesters*
[2] *allow me to take some evidence so that your wife will pay me*
[3] *you've taken this joke too far*
[4] *my business is urgent; I can't tolerate this time-wasting*

Eventually the merchant, running out of patience, tells Antipholus that he must pay the outstanding sum: failing that, the goldsmith will be arrested for failure to pay his debt. Antipholus, denying again that he has received the chain, refuses to pay, and the officer places Angelo under arrest.

> *... you know I gave it to you even now.*
>
> "Not only does public time seem to have gone awry, but the inner time-sense of the protagonists, their notion of 'before', 'after' and 'now', has become seriously deranged ... no one in the play is able to give a reliable account of the present or the immediate past."
>
> Gamini Salgado, *Time's Deformed Hand*, 1972

Angelo, in turn, pays the officer his fee, and orders him to arrest Antipholus. He is furious that his reputation for honest dealing has been called into question. Antipholus retorts that, once he has paid bail to secure his release, he will sue the goldsmith for all he is worth:

Angelo: ... arrest him, officer.
 I would not spare my brother in this case
 If he should scorn me so apparently.[1]
Officer: I do arrest you, sir; you hear the suit.[2]
Antipholus of Ephesus: I do obey thee till I give thee bail.
 [*to Angelo*] But, sirrah, you shall buy this sport as dear
 As all the metal in your shop will answer.[3]
Angelo: Sir, sir, I shall have law [4] in Ephesus ...

[1] *slander me so blatantly*
[2] *you have heard the charges against you*
[3] *this mischief will cost you all the gold in your shop*
[4] *justice*

Just as Antipholus is arrested, Dromio rushes into the marketplace. But this is not the Dromio just sent off to buy a rope; it is Dromio of Syracuse, sent to the dockside to enquire about departures. He has good news for his master: a ship is ready and waiting, and all their baggage is on board. The owner is already on his way to the harbour:

Dromio of Syracuse: The ship is in her trim;[1] the merry wind
 Blows fair from land: they stay for naught at all [2]
 But for their owner, master, and yourself.

[1] *fully rigged, ready to set sail*
[2] *the crew are not waiting for anything else*

Antipholus has no idea why his servant is prattling about ships and sailing; no doubt the man has been drinking again. However, he is in no mood to argue at the moment.

43

As Antipholus is led away to prison, he gives Dromio a key, instructing him to run back to the Phoenix and get enough money for his release:

Antipholus of Ephesus: To Adriana, villain, hie thee straight:[1]
　　　　　　　　Give her this key, and tell her, in the desk
　　　　　　　　That's covered o'er with Turkish tapestry,
　　　　　　　　There is a purse of ducats:[2] let her send it.
　　　　　　　　Tell her I am arrested in the street
　　　　　　　　And that shall bail me. Hie thee, slave. Be gone!

　　　[1] *hurry at once*
　　　[2] *gold coins*

Dromio realises, with dismay, that Adriana's house is also the home of the fearsome kitchen maid, Nell, who claims to be his wife. Nevertheless, orders must be obeyed, he tells himself, and he reluctantly sets off.

Mixed feelings　　　　　　　　　　　　　　　　　　　IV, ii

Following her alarming encounter with the love-struck Antipholus, Luciana is confiding in her sister. Adriana questions her closely: how did he look? Was he serious or light-hearted in his attempt to seduce her? Luciana tells her, truthfully, that he behaved as though his marriage to Adriana meant nothing:

Luciana:	First he denied you had in him no right.[1]
Adriana:	He meant he did me none; the more my spite.[2]
Luciana:	Then swore he that he was a stranger here.
Adriana:	And true he swore, though yet forsworn he were.[3]
Luciana:	Then pleaded I for you.
Adriana:	And what said he?
Luciana:	That love I begged for you, he begged of me.[4]

　　　[1] *he said you had no rights over him*
　　　[2] *the fact is he never does right by me; that's what is making me unhappy*
　　　[3] *even though he was lying, it's true that he behaves like a stranger*
　　　[4] *when I asked him to express his love for you, he asked me to tell him I loved him*

Adriana, growing increasingly angry and unhappy, hints that her sister may have encouraged Antipholus. When Luciana urges her to remain calm, Adriana cannot contain her feelings about her unfaithful husband any longer:

Luciana: Have patience, I beseech.
Adriana: I cannot, nor I will not, hold me still;
My tongue, though not my heart, shall have his will.[1]
He is deformed, crooked, old and sere,[2]
Ill-faced, worse bodied,[3] shapeless everywhere;
Vicious, ungentle, foolish, blunt, unkind,
Stigmatical in making,[4] worse in mind.

[1] *although I cannot have what I desire, I shall say what I feel*
[2] *withered, dried up*
[3] *his face is ugly, and his body even more so*
[4] *cursed with physical deformity*

Luciana, taking her sister's words at face value, suggests that she should not feel jealous if she finds Antipholus so unappealing. Her emotions are not as simple as that, Adriana confesses; deep down, she is still devoted to her husband.

At this moment, Dromio rushes in, carrying the key given to him by his master. He tries to convey the fact that Antipholus has been detained, but at first the women can make no sense of his breathless gabbling:

Dromio of Syracuse: ... he's in Tartar limbo,[1] worse than hell:
A devil in an everlasting garment hath him,
One whose hard heart is buttoned up with steel;
A fiend, a fairy,[2] pitiless and rough;
A wolf, nay, worse, a fellow all in buff[3] ...

[1] *Tartarus; the deep, hellish pit of Greek mythology, where the wicked were punished for their misdeeds*
[2] *a supernatural being*
[3] *the bailiff's thick leather coat*

Eventually it becomes clear that Antipholus has been arrested, and needs money if he is to avoid going to prison. Adriana tries to establish what crime he has committed, but Dromio's mention of the necklace means nothing to her. The striking of a clock adds to the confusion:

> *Adriana:* This I wonder at,
> That he unknown to me should be in debt.
> Tell me, was he arrested on a bond?[1]
> *Dromio of Syracuse:* Not on a bond, but on a stronger thing:
> A chain, a chain – do you not hear it ring?
> *Adriana:* What, the chain?
> *Dromio of Syracuse:* No, no, the bell; 'tis time that I were gone ...
>
> [1] *written obligation to repay a debt*

Luciana fetches Antipholus's purse, and Adriana, by now emotionally exhausted, sends Dromio away to pay his master's bail and bring him safely home.

A visitation IV, iii

Antipholus of Syracuse has come to the marketplace, hoping that his servant will bring news of ships due to leave Ephesus. He is mystified by the attention he is receiving from strangers. Everyone here seems to know him:

> *Antipholus of Syracuse:* There's not a man I meet but doth salute me[1]
> As if I were their well-acquainted friend,
> And everyone doth call me by my name.
> Some tender money to me; some invite me;
> Some other give me thanks for kindnesses;
> Some offer me commodities to buy.
>
> [1] *everyone I come across stops to greet me*

"*The prosaic, day-to-day business of a commercial town becomes something strange and dreamlike, because it is all happening to the wrong man.*"

Alexander Leggatt, *Shakespeare's Comedy of Love*, 1974

Finding the experience unsettling, Antipholus decides that his imagination is playing tricks on him; sorcery is clearly at work in this city. His mood is not helped when Dromio appears and unaccountably hands him a purse full of gold coins. His servant then comes up with an odd, incomprehensible story about an arresting officer: and, to make things worse, the man claims that he has already told Antipholus about a ship that is shortly to depart.

The confusion is becoming intolerable, and Antipholus prays out loud to be released from the nightmarish world in which he now finds himself:

Antipholus of Syracuse: The fellow is distract,[1] and so am I,
    And here we wander in illusions –
    Some blessed power deliver us from hence![2]

    [1] *deranged, perplexed*
    [2] *rescue us from this place*

Antipholus is still wearing the gold chain given to him recently by a stranger. When an attractive young woman approaches, addresses him warmly and asks for the chain, Antipholus, already on edge, falls into a blind panic, convinced that evil supernatural forces are closing in on him:

Courtesan: Well met, well met, Master Antipholus.
    I see, sir, you have found the goldsmith now:
    Is that the chain you promised me today?
Antipholus of Syracuse: Satan, avoid![1] I charge[2] thee, tempt me not!
Dromio of Syracuse: Master, is this Mistress Satan?
Antipholus of Syracuse: It is the devil.

    [1] *get away from me*
    [2] *command*

The courtesan is amused: Adriana's husband is obviously playing some prank or other. She indicates her house, the Porcupine, and suggests that they go back there to finish the lunch that they started earlier:

Courtesan: Your man and you are marvellous merry, sir.
Will you go with me? We'll mend[1] our dinner here.

[1] *finish off*

Antipholus frantically tries to ward off the demonic apparition. The courtesan refuses to leave him alone, however: she claims that he has something belonging to her. In the Porcupine, it transpires, she gave her companion a diamond ring in exchange for the promise of a gold chain. If she cannot have the chain, it is only fair that she should get her ring back:

Antipholus of Syracuse: Thou art, as you are all, a sorceress;
I conjure[1] thee to leave me and be gone.
Courtesan: Give me the ring of mine you had at dinner,
Or for my diamond the chain you promised,
And I'll be gone, sir, and not trouble you.

[1] *beg, beseech*

Unable to rid themselves of this enchantress, Antipholus and Dromio make a hasty exit. The courtesan decides that there can only be one reason for her friend's scandalous behaviour:

Courtesan: Now, out of doubt,[1] Antipholus is mad,
Else would he never so demean himself.[2]
A ring he hath of mine worth forty ducats,
And for the same he promised me a chain;
Both one and other he denies me now.

[1] *without a doubt, unquestionably*
[2] *he would never behave so disgracefully otherwise*

It occurs to her that Antipholus told her a strange story at lunchtime, claiming that his wife had locked him out of his own house. She now realises that Adriana was acting in self-defence; clearly these spells of insanity are a regular occurrence. Adriana must be told of her husband's latest escapade, she decides, with a little embellishment if necessary. Her ring was valuable, and she cannot afford to lose it:

Courtesan: My way is now to hie home to his house [1]
And tell his wife that, being lunatic,
He rushed into my house and took perforce
My ring away.[2] This course I fittest choose,[3]
For forty ducats is too much to lose.

[1] *what I shall do now is hurry over to his house*
[2] *violently stole my ring from me*
[3] *this is the most appropriate course to take*

... I conjure thee to leave me and be gone.

Many Shakespearean plays are given their unique character and atmosphere through the repetition of certain key words, images and ideas. In *The Comedy of Errors*, for example, the words 'conjure' and 'conjuror' (with the sense of appealing to or exorcising evil spirits) appear more often than in any other Shakespeare play. Other words relating to the supernatural – such as 'witch', 'sorcery' and 'devil' – also occur frequently, as do their positive counterparts, 'holy' and 'divine'.

The characters' spiritual and emotional confusion is played out against the background of a busy centre of trade and commerce, sketched in by recurrent mentions of 'merchants', 'gold', 'ducats' and related words. And even though *The Comedy of Errors* is his shortest play, Shakespeare uses the word 'money' more frequently here than anywhere else.

An unwilling patient
IV, iv

Antipholus of Ephesus, meanwhile, is on his way to prison. He assures the arresting officer that he will not attempt to escape. His wife, despite the perverse mood that she seems to be in today, will no doubt be shocked to hear of his arrest. Any minute now, she will send their servant back with enough money to cover the alleged debt owed to the goldsmith.

Antipholus is relieved to see his servant approaching. This, however, is Dromio of Ephesus returning from his errand; his master, determined to punish Adriana, had sent him off earlier to buy a rope. Antipholus is appalled as Dromio proudly reveals his purchase:

Antipholus of Ephesus: Here comes my man; I think he brings the money.
[*to Dromio*] How now, sir? Have you that I sent you for?
Dromio of Ephesus: [*offering the rope*] Here's that, I warrant you, will pay them all.[1]
Antipholus of Ephesus: But where's the money?
Dromio of Ephesus: Why, sir, I gave the money for the rope.
Antipholus of Ephesus: Five hundred ducats, villain, for a rope?

[1] *here's the thing which, I promise, will enable you to get your revenge*

Furious that his servant has spent a purse full of gold coins on a piece of rope, Antipholus seizes the rope and thrashes Dromio mercilessly, ignoring the officer's pleas for patience. As he runs around trying to avoid the blows, Dromio complains that his master, whom he has served all his life, frequently beats him for no reason:

Dromio of Ephesus: … I have served him from the hour of my nativity to this instant and have nothing at his hands for my service but blows. When I am cold, he heats me with beating; when I am warm, he cools me with beating. I am waked with it when I sleep, raised with it when I sit, driven out of doors with it when I go from home, welcomed home with it when I return.

Adriana and Luciana now arrive on the scene, accompanied by the courtesan, who has just reported Antipholus's apparent madness and his theft of her diamond ring. They have brought Doctor Pinch, who claims to be an expert in dealing with mental instability and demonic possession.

The scene that greets them confirms the courtesan's claims, as Antipholus chases his servant around the marketplace, lashing out wildly with a piece of rope. Adriana asks the doctor to do whatever he can to restore her husband's sanity, regardless of the cost:

Courtesan: How say you now?[1] Is not your husband mad?
Adriana: His incivility confirms no less.[2]
Good Doctor Pinch, you are a conjuror:[3]
Establish him in his true sense again,
And I will please you what you will demand.
Luciana: Alas, how fiery and how sharp he looks!
Courtesan: Mark how he trembles in his ecstasy.[4]

[1] *now do you see what I mean?*
[2] *his unruly behaviour proves it*
[3] *an exorcist, one who can banish evil spirits*
[4] *fit of madness, frenzy*

Antipholus does not welcome Pinch's attention, and the doctor concludes that the devil is at work:

Pinch: Give me your hand, and let me feel your pulse.
Antipholus of Ephesus: [*striking Pinch*] There is my hand, and let it feel your ear.
Pinch: I charge thee, Satan, housed within this man,
To yield possession to my holy prayers,
And to thy state of darkness hie thee straight;[1]
I conjure thee by all the saints in heaven.
Antipholus of Ephesus: Peace,[2] doting[3] wizard, peace; I am not mad.
Adriana: O, that thou wert not,[4] poor distressed soul.

[1] *get back to your evil abode at once*
[2] *be quiet*
[3] *senile, doddering*
[4] *I wish you weren't*

51

The accusations fly

Hearing his wife's voice, Antipholus condemns her angrily: at lunchtime, she was no doubt entertaining this Doctor Pinch at the Phoenix while making sure that her own husband was out of the way. Adriana, distressed at his obvious derangement, insists that she had lunch with Antipholus:

Antipholus of Ephesus: Did this companion with the saffron[1] face
　　　　　　　　　Revel and feast it at my house today,
　　　　　　　　　Whilst upon me the guilty doors were shut,
　　　　　　　　　And I denied[2] to enter in my house?
Adriana:　　　O husband, God doth know you dined at home,
　　　　　　　　　Where would you had remained until this time,
　　　　　　　　　Free from these slanders and this open shame.[3]

　　[1] *yellow; sickly, ageing*
　　[2] *forbidden*
　　[3] *where I wish you had remained all afternoon, avoiding this insulting language and public humiliation*

Antipholus turns to his servant to back him up. Dromio of Ephesus, who like his master was locked out of the house, agrees: Antipholus did not have lunch at home. He goes on to confirm the rest of his master's story. As well as being shut out, Antipholus was insulted by the servants inside the house, and even his wife told him in no uncertain terms to go away.

Adriana wonders whether Dromio should go along with his master's delusions in this way. He is doing exactly the right thing, declares the doctor:

Adriana:　Is't good to soothe him in these contraries?[1]
Pinch:　　It is no shame: the fellow finds his vein[2]
　　　　　　And, yielding to him, humours well his frenzy.[3]

　　[1] *is it a good idea to humour him when he makes up these stories?*
　　[2] *the man has understood his master's frame of mind*
　　[3] *is keeping his madness under control by agreeing with everything he says*

When Antipholus accuses her of colluding in his arrest, Adriana points out that, on the contrary, she provided the money for his release: she gave it to Dromio not long ago. Dromio denies all knowledge of the money, stating that his master sent him away for nothing more than a piece of rope.

Antipholus, Adriana and Luciana all turn on Dromio, who is clearly lying. There can only be one explanation, Doctor Pinch tells Adriana confidently, and one remedy:

> Pinch: Mistress, both man and master[1] is possessed:
> I know it by their pale and deadly looks.
> They must be bound and laid in some dark room.
>
> [1] *Dromio and Antipholus*

Susanna Shakespeare, the oldest of William's three children, was ten when her father wrote *The Comedy of Errors*. At the age of twenty-four, she would go on to marry John Hall, a physician who had set up a practice in Stratford-upon-Avon.

The world of medicine at the time was rife with frauds, charlatans and tricksters, and was not generally held in high esteem. However, the relationship between Shakespeare and his son-in-law seems to have been one of mutual warmth and respect. Did Doctor Hall, with his methodical, scientific approach and high ethical standards, change his father-in-law's view of the profession?

"We must always be wary of attempts to map Shakespeare's life on to his work. But writers cannot avoid drawing on their experience. Is it a coincidence that in Shakespeare's earlier works there are two comic doctors – including Pinch in The Comedy of Errors *– whereas in the plays written after John Hall's arrival in Stratford-upon-Avon, there are several dignified, sympathetically portrayed medical men?"*

Jonathan Bate, *Soul of the Age*, 2008

Antipholus wants to know, above all, why his wife locked him out and why his servant has not brought the money. Both deny the accusations, trying to pacify him at the same time:

> *Antipholus of Ephesus:* [*to Adriana*] Say wherefore didst thou lock me forth[1] today?
> [*to Dromio*] And why dost thou deny the bag of gold?
> *Adriana:* I did not, gentle husband, lock thee forth.
> *Dromio of Ephesus:* And, gentle master, I received no gold,
> But I confess,[2] sir, that we were locked out.
>
> [1] *why did you lock me out of the house*
> [2] *agree*

Their attempt to calm the situation down, however, has the opposite effect. Adriana is furious that Dromio is both lying about the gold she gave him and pretending that he was locked out of the house. Antipholus, equally enraged, decides that his wife is at the centre of a malicious plot to make a fool of him:

> *Adriana:* [*to Dromio*] Dissembling[1] villain, thou speak'st false in both.
> *Antipholus of Ephesus:* Dissembling harlot, thou art false in all,
> And art confederate[2] with a damned pack
> To make a loathsome, abject scorn[3] of me;
> But with these nails I'll pluck out those false[4] eyes
> That would behold in me this shameful sport.
>
> [1] *lying*
> [2] *in league, in collusion*
> [3] *mockery, laughing stock*
> [4] *deceitful, spiteful*

With that, Antipholus lunges forward, threatening to lash out at his wife.

> *"In contrast to his brother, Antipholus of Ephesus is always seen in the company of men only – his servant, friends, business associates, creditors ... until the conjuring (exorcism) scene, when at last he is surrounded by women – his wife, his sister-in-law, the Courtesan – who insist that he is mad."*
>
> Charles Whitworth, Introduction to the Oxford Shakespeare edition of *The Comedy of Errors*, 2002

A violent outburst

Adriana cries out in terror, calling for Antipholus to be restrained. Pinch shouts out for support, and several of his assistants rush in. A struggle ensues as they set upon Antipholus and attempt to tie him up. As Pinch observes, it is not an easy task; the demon possessing his patient is particularly tenacious. Luciana sympathises with Adriana's unfortunate husband:

Adriana:	O, bind him, bind him! Let him not come near me!
Pinch:	More company!
	[*Three or four men come in and attempt to bind Antipholus, who resists.*]
	The fiend is strong within him.
Luciana:	Ay me, poor man, how pale and wan[1] he looks.

[1] *ashen, deathly*

Antipholus calls out to the arresting officer, who has been standing aside during the whole disturbance. The man appeals ineffectually for his prisoner to be left alone, but Pinch and his helpers ignore his request. Once they have tied Antipholus up, they turn their attention to Dromio.

Adriana, distressed to see her husband in this state, also rounds angrily on the officer, who insists that Antipholus must be kept in custody until his debt is paid. Adriana gives her word that she will pay whatever is due. She tells Doctor Pinch to take her husband back to the Phoenix, and Antipholus and Dromio, now securely tied up, are escorted away.

Armed and dangerous

With the indignant master and his servant safely removed, peace finally descends on the scene. Adriana questions the officer about her husband's arrest, and he explains that it concerns an unpaid debt to Angelo, the goldsmith.

Adriana remembers that her husband had asked Angelo to make a necklace for her, but as far as she knows the goldsmith has not yet delivered it. The courtesan mentions that Antipholus visited her at lunchtime and took her ring; in fact, he is still wearing it. He was already in a deranged state, she claims, and soon afterwards she saw him wearing the gold chain himself:

Adriana: He did bespeak a chain[1] for me, but had it not.
Courtesan: Whenas[2] your husband all in rage today
 Came to my house and took away my ring –
 The ring I saw upon his finger now –
 Straight after did I meet him with a chain.
Adriana: It may be so, but I did never see it.

[1] *arrange for a chain to be made*
[2] *when*

Hoping that the matter can be resolved, Adriana asks the officer to go with her to Angelo's shop. Just as they turn to leave, though, they are confronted with a terrifying sight. Antipholus and Dromio, having apparently broken free from their bonds and escaped from the house, are coming towards them menacingly: and this time they are armed.

Adriana, her sister, the officer and the courtesan all run for their lives, screaming for help:

Luciana: God, for thy mercy! They are loose again.
Adriana: And come with naked[1] swords! Let's call more help
 To have them bound again.
Officer: Away, they'll kill us!

[1] *unsheathed, drawn*

Time to move on

Antipholus of Syracuse is pleased: the assorted spirits, sorcerers and devils that inhabit this city can clearly be scared off, like ordinary mortals, with a show of force.

After his experience with the she-devil who demanded his gold chain, he has decided to keep his rapier drawn, and it has just had the desired effect. Even the woman who claimed to be married to him has run off in fright:

> *Antipholus of Syracuse:* I see these witches are afraid of swords.
> *Dromio of Syracuse:* She that would be[1] your wife now ran from you.
>
> [1] *pretended to be*

Unaware of their identical twins, still bound up and confined to the Phoenix under the care of Doctor Pinch, Antipholus and Dromio discuss their next step.

Dromio is tempted by the idea of staying longer; in fact, were it not for the presence of Nell the kitchen maid, he would happily settle down here, regardless of the supernatural goings-on. Antipholus disagrees, insisting that they must leave as soon as possible, without staying a single night:

> *Dromio of Syracuse:* Faith, stay here this night; they will surely do
>   us no harm. You saw they speak us fair, give us gold:
>   methinks they are such a gentle nation that, but for the
>   mountain of mad flesh that claims marriage of me, I
>   could find in my heart to stay here still and turn witch.[1]
> *Antipholus of Syracuse:* I will not stay tonight for all the town;[2]
>   Therefore, away, to get our stuff aboard.[3]
>
> [1] *stay here permanently, and become one of the locals*
> [2] *for all the wealth in Ephesus*
> [3] *on board ship, ready to depart*

The chain reappears V, i

Angelo is talking to the merchant who, earlier, had requested urgent repayment of a debt. Angelo is mystified by the behaviour of his customer Antipholus. In the past, the tells the merchant, Antipholus has always been renowned throughout the city for his honesty and good character:

Angelo: I am sorry, sir, that I have hindered[1] you,
            But I protest he had the chain of me,[2]
            Though most dishonestly he doth deny it.
Merchant: How is the man esteemed here in the city?
Angelo: Of very reverend[3] reputation, sir,
            Of credit infinite, highly beloved,
            Second to none that lives here in the city;
            His word might bear my wealth at any time.[4]

> [1] *troubled, delayed*
> [2] *I swear that I gave him the chain*
> [3] *respected*
> [4] *I would happily lend all my wealth if I had his word as security*

At this moment, Antipholus and Dromio of Syracuse, on their way to the harbour, pass by. Angelo is incensed to see that Antipholus is wearing a gold chain, the same chain that he claimed not to have received. It was his refusal to pay for it that has caused so much distress all round. The goldsmith confronts him:

Angelo: Signor Antipholus, I wonder much[1]
            That you would put me to this shame and trouble,
            And not without some scandal to yourself,
            With circumstance and oaths so to deny
            This chain[2] which now you wear so openly.

> [1] *I am amazed*
> [2] *by giving complicated excuses and sworn denials, and claiming that you never received the chain*

58

His denial, Angelo tells him, has resulted in shame for himself, and inconvenience and embarrassment for others. The merchant by his side, moreover, was unable to set out on his voyage as planned due to Antipholus's failure to pay his debt.

Antipholus is nonplussed. He remembers receiving the gold chain perfectly well, and has never denied having it. The merchant interjects: earlier, Antipholus claimed many times over that he had not received the chain. A quarrel quickly breaks out between the two men:

Merchant: These ears of mine, thou knowst, did hear thee.
Fie on thee, wretch! 'Tis pity that thou liv'st
To walk where any honest men resort.
Antipholus of Syracuse: Thou art a villain to impeach[1] me thus!
I'll prove mine honour and mine honesty
Against thee presently,[2] if thou dar'st stand.[3]
Merchant: I dare, and do defy thee for a villain!
[*They draw their swords.*]

[1] *accuse*
[2] *immediately*
[3] *make a stand, fight*

> "*The Comedy of Errors is saturated with merchants; the comedy's backdrop is a trade war; a luxury commodity, gold, plays a key role in the plot; and an international trader's urgency to collect a debt spurs the action into crisis.*"
>
> Kent Cartwright, Introduction to the Arden Shakespeare edition of *The Comedy of Errors*, 2016

Just as the two men face up to one another, Adriana returns, along with Luciana and the courtesan. Scared away a few minutes ago by the sudden appearance of Antipholus brandishing his sword, they have armed themselves with ropes in order to capture Adriana's unfortunate, deluded husband and tie him up securely. Adriana urges the merchant not to attack him:

Adriana: Hold,[1] hurt him not, for God's sake; he is mad!
Some get within him,[2] take his sword away.
Bind Dromio too, and bear them to my house.

[1] *stop, wait*
[2] *within his guard, close to him*

Outnumbered, Antipholus and Dromio decide to beat a hasty retreat. Dromio spots an abbey nearby, and the two men hurriedly take sanctuary inside.

A case of jealousy

A few seconds later, the abbey door opens and the abbess, head of the community of nuns within, emerges. She asks what has brought about this rowdy assembly:

Abbess: Be quiet, people. Wherefore throng you hither?[1]
Adriana: To fetch my poor distracted husband hence;[2]
Let us come in, that we may bind him fast[3]
And bear him home for his recovery.

[1] *why are you all gathering here?*
[2] *from here*
[3] *securely*

At first, the abbess does not address Adriana's request. Instead, she questions her closely about her husband's distress. Adriana explains that, although he has been moody in recent days, it is only today that his violent mental turmoil has become apparent:

Abbess: How long hath this possession¹ held the man?
Adriana: This week he hath been heavy, sour, sad,
And much different from the man he was;
But till this afternoon his passion
Ne'er broke into extremity of rage.²

¹ *madness; control by a malicious spirit*
² *his emotions didn't erupt into furious aggression*

Responding to the abbess's enquiries, she confesses that she suspects Antipholus of infidelity:

Abbess: Hath he not lost much wealth by wrack of sea?¹
Buried some dear friend? Hath not else his eye
Strayed his affection in unlawful love?² –
A sin prevailing much in youthful men …
Adriana: To none of these, except³ it be the last,
Namely, some love that drew him oft from home.

¹ *lost a fortune in a shipwreck*
² *led his feelings astray, in the direction of infidelity*
³ *unless*

The abbess persists with her questions: perhaps Adriana was not forceful enough in pursuing the subject, she suggests. Growing impatient, Adriana responds vehemently, and insists that she has talked of little else recently; her misgivings about Antipholus's fidelity have been at the forefront of all their conversations. Unwittingly, though, she has confirmed the abbess's suspicions:

Adriana: It was the copy of our conference:¹
In bed he slept not for my urging it;
At board² he fed not for my urging it;
Alone, it was the subject of my theme;
In company I often glanced at³ it;
Still⁴ did I tell him it was vile and bad.
Abbess: And thereof came it that the man was mad …

¹ *the subject-matter of our discussions*
² *mealtimes*
³ *mentioned, referred to*
⁴ *continually*

Antipholus has clearly been unable to sleep, eat, relax, or take pleasure in anything, claims the abbess. In, short, he has been driven to distraction by Adriana's obsessive jealousy.

Luciana is outraged; her sister's behaviour has been much more reasonable than her husband's. Adriana herself, however, does not respond. She suspects, deep down, that the abbess may be right:

Abbess:	… The consequence is, then, thy jealous fits
	Hath scared thy husband from the use of wits.
Luciana:	She never reprehended him but mildly,[1]
	When he demeaned himself rough, rude and wildly.[2]
	[*to Adriana*] Why bear you these rebukes and answer not?
Adriana:	She did betray me to my own reproof.[3]

> [1] *she only reprimanded him mildly*
> [2] *he behaved disgracefully and aggressively*
> [3] *she has confirmed my own criticism of myself*

A fateful hour

Changing the subject, Adriana now asks her companions to go into the abbey and find her husband. The abbess resolutely refuses to allow anyone to enter. Antipholus has come to her abbey seeking protection, and it is her responsibility to look after him. She will do her utmost to restore his well-being:

Adriana:	… Good people, enter and lay hold on him.
Abbess:	No, not a creature enters in my house.
Adriana:	Then let your servants bring my husband forth.
Abbess:	Neither. He took this place for sanctuary,[1]
	And it shall privilege him from your hands[2]
	Till I have brought him to his wits again
	Or lose my labour in assaying it.[3]

> [1] *official protection offered by the Church*
> [2] *that means he is not subject to your authority*
> [3] *or, in attempting to cure him, reach the limit of my abilities*

The two women quickly come to a stalemate: the abbess refuses to let Adriana see her husband, while Adriana, believing that it is her responsibility to look after him, refuses to leave. Luciana suggests to her sister that she should appeal to the Duke of Ephesus. Adriana agrees, confident that she can persuade him to have her husband released from the abbey. They must make their way to his palace immediately, she announces.

At this point the merchant cuts in. The duke is probably on his way to the abbey at this very moment, he reveals. The time at which executions are carried out is approaching, and the place of beheading is not far from the abbey:

Merchant: By this, I think, the dial points at five;[1]
Anon,[2] I'm sure, the Duke himself in person
Comes this way to the melancholy vale,
The place of death and sorry execution,
Behind the ditches of the abbey here.

[1] *it is probably five o'clock by now*
[2] *soon*

By this, I think, the dial points at five ...

There are more references to time in *The Comedy of Errors* than in any other Shakespearean comedy. The action of the play takes place in a single afternoon, and the frequent mentions of time and its passing remind us that a crucial deadline is approaching:

"*Even at his most comic, Shakespeare cannot resist allowing more serious themes of cruelty and death to seep through the comic fabric* ... The Comedy of Errors *is played out beneath the threat of execution.*"

Catharine Arnold, *Globe: Life in Shakespeare's London*, 2015

The merchant goes on to explain that an elderly man is to be put to death; the man is a Syracusan, and his presence in Ephesus is therefore outlawed. As the merchant is speaking, the duke appears, followed by the convicted offender, accompanied by the duke's officers and the executioner.

The condemned man is Egeon, whose search for his lost son brought him, by chance, to Ephesus. The duke repeats his earlier wish that enough money might be raised to pay Egeon's ransom and save his life. Since hearing his story earlier today, the duke has felt increasingly sympathetic towards the old man, who has wandered so far on his arduous quest:

Duke: Yet once again proclaim it publicly,
If any friend will pay the sum for him,
He shall not die, so much we tender him.[1]

[1] *because we hold him so dear*

Before anyone can respond to the duke's proclamation, Adriana comes forward and kneels before him. She makes an impassioned plea, one which surprises the duke:

Adriana: Justice, most sacred Duke, against the abbess!
Duke: She is a virtuous and a reverend lady;
It cannot be that she hath done thee wrong.

Adriana now summarises her case. She starts by reminding the duke that he helped to arrange her marriage to Antipholus, and goes on to describe the bout of insanity that has suddenly afflicted her husband. The courtesan's claim that he snatched her diamond ring from her has grown into a much more sensational, dramatic story:

Adriana: ... this ill day,
A most outrageous fit of madness took him,
That[1] desp'rately he hurried through the street,
With him his bondman, all as mad as he,[2]
Doing displeasure to the citizens
By rushing in their houses, bearing thence
Rings, jewels, anything his rage did like.[3]

[1] *with the result that*
[2] *accompanied by his servant, who was just as mad as him*
[3] *stealing whatever he felt like in his fury*

The two men were tied up and taken home, she reports, but somehow managed to escape. They then ran amok, wielding their swords, but were eventually forced to flee, taking refuge in the abbey. She implores the duke to allow her to have her husband back, so that she can look after him.

Long ago, the duke remembers, Antipholus was of great service to him. At that time, the duke promised to help him and his wife in any way he could:

Adriana: ... most gracious Duke, with thy command,
Let him be brought forth and borne hence[1] for help.
Duke: Long since, thy husband served me in my wars,
And I to thee engaged a prince's word,[2]
When thou didst make him master of thy bed,[3]
To do him all the grace and good I could.

[1] *taken away from the abbey*
[2] *gave you my word as ruler*
[3] *when you consented to marry him*

The duke decides to talk to the abbess; this matter must be settled, he announces, before any other business – including the execution of Egeon – can go ahead.

> *"Where some of his early shows seem over-wordy to a modern audience,* The Comedy of Errors *still works a treat with its helter-skelter action based on the mistaken identity of two sets of twins (the father of twins himself, Shakespeare made twins the central characters in two of his plays, and pulled it off). Some of the key plot ideas are particularly interesting: shipwrecks, storms, personal loss, parents and children, the reuniting of a family; the potential of tragedy in comedy. These were the themes to which he would return compulsively all his life."*
>
> Michael Wood, *In Search of Shakespeare*, 2005

Contradictions

A messenger suddenly rushes in from the Phoenix, urging Adriana to run away immediately. He warns her that, incredibly, Antipholus and Dromio are loose yet again. They have tied up Doctor Pinch, set fire to his beard, and clipped his hair to make him look ridiculous, mocking him cruelly all the while.

Adriana tells the messenger not to talk nonsense: her husband is inside the abbey with his servant. The man insists that Antipholus is on his way as they speak, and is intent on tracking her down:

Messenger: ... sure, unless you send some present[1] help,
 Between them they will kill the conjuror.[2]
Adriana: Peace,[3] fool; thy master and his man are here,
 And that is false thou dost report to us.
Messenger: Mistress, upon my life, I tell you true;
 I have not breathed almost since I did see it.
 He cries for you and vows, if he can take[4] you,
 To scorch your face and to disfigure you.

[1] *immediate*
[2] *the exorcist; Doctor Pinch*
[3] *be quiet*
[4] *catch*

No sooner has the man finished speaking than commotion breaks out in the marketplace as Antipholus and Dromio charge angrily onto the scene, just as the messenger had warned. The duke calls Adriana to his side, and orders his men to draw their weapons and form a defensive ring around them. Adriana, transfixed, cannot believe her eyes. Supernatural powers are clearly in action:

> *Adriana:* Ay me, it is my husband! Witness you
> That he is borne about invisible:[1]
> Even[2] now we housed him in the abbey here,
> And now he's there, past thought of human reason.
>
> [1] *he is carried around by invisible forces*
> [2] *just*

Unaware of his twin brother hiding in the abbey, Antipholus cries out passionately for justice. He dramatically reminds the duke that he once saved his ruler's life:

> *Antipholus of Ephesus:* Justice, most gracious Duke! O, grant me justice,
> Even for the service that long since I did thee,
> When I bestrid thee[1] in the wars and took
> Deep scars to save thy life ...
>
> [1] *stood over you protectively when you were down*

Egeon, looking on as he awaits execution, is convinced that he recognises the two intruders:

> *Egeon:* [*aside*] Unless the fear of death doth make me dote,[1]
> I see my son Antipholus and Dromio.
>
> [1] *has driven me insane*

Pressing on with his plea for justice, Antipholus denounces his wife. Earlier today, he insists, she locked him out of his own house. Adriana denies the charge, and her sister adds her voice: Antipholus had lunch with them, in their home.

The goldsmith Angelo adds to the confusion: he knows that Antipholus was indeed locked out of his house, so the two women cannot be telling the truth. On the other hand, Antipholus's strange insistence that he never received the gold chain confirms that he is not in his right mind:

Angelo: They are both forsworn:[1]
In this the madman justly chargeth them.[2]

[1] *Adriana and Luciana are both lying*
[2] *Antipholus's accusation is true, even though he is mad*

Antipholus maintains that he is perfectly sane, and is telling the truth about all the day's events:

Antipholus of Ephesus: My liege, I am advised what I say,[1]
Neither disturbed with the effect of wine,
Nor heady-rash, provoked with raging ire,
Albeit my wrongs might make one wiser mad.[2]

[1] *I am choosing my words carefully*
[2] *even though the injustices done to me would be enough to drive a wiser man than me mad*

He goes on to recount his misfortunes. After having lunch with a friend, he met Angelo and a merchant, who demanded money from him even though he had not received his promised gold chain; they eventually had him arrested. His servant, sent away to fetch money for his bail, came back with nothing. His wife then enlisted the help of a fraudster by the name of Pinch who, along with his assistants, assaulted him, tied him up and dragged him home, where he was dumped in a cellar. Antipholus reveals that he had to take extreme measures in order to escape:

Antipholus of Ephesus: ... They fell upon me, bound me, bore me thence,[1]
And in a dark and dankish vault at home
There left me and my man, both bound together,
Till, gnawing with my teeth my bonds in sunder,[2]
I gained my freedom ...

[1] *carried me away*
[2] *gnawing through the ropes with which I was bound*

For some reason everyone around him is lying, claims Antipholus. He repeats, in exasperation, that he did not dine with his wife, never received the chain, did not draw his sword on anyone, and has never been inside the abbey.

The duke attempts to unravel the various stories from the different participants, but without success:

> Duke: [*to the merchant*] If here you housed him, here he would have been;[1]
> [*to Adriana*] If he were mad, he would not plead so coldly;[2]
> [*to Luciana*] You say he dined at home; the goldsmith here denies that saying.
>
> [1] *if you had put him in the abbey, he would still be there*
> [2] *he would not argue his case so rationally*

In Shakespeare's time, play scripts were the property of the theatre company for which they were written. They were a valuable asset, and companies were generally unwilling to publish them, particularly while a play was still popular and attracting audiences. At least half of Shakespeare's plays, for example, were not published during his lifetime.

In time, however, plays gradually came to be regarded, like poetry, as valid works of literature. Five years after Shakespeare's death, John Heminges and Henry Condell, two of his fellow-actors, set about the task of creating a complete edition of Shakespeare's plays, including introductory material and an engraving of the author. The resulting book, now known as the 'First Folio', was published in 1623. This collected edition contained many plays – including *The Tempest*, *Macbeth*, *Twelfth Night* and *The Comedy of Errors* – which would otherwise have been lost for ever.

The duke addresses Dromio, who in turn mentions the courtesan. She confirms that Antipholus had lunch with her, and took her ring, which he is now wearing; she too, though, saw him enter the abbey. Only one person can help, decides the duke: he calls again for the abbess to be brought before him.

A final plea

One of the duke's attendants sets off for the abbey, and the competing claims of the various individuals come to an inconclusive standstill. Egeon takes the opportunity to speak out. If his intuition proves true, he will be reunited with his son, and his life will be saved into the bargain:

Egeon: Most mighty Duke, vouchsafe me[1] speak a word;
Haply[2] I see a friend will save my life
And pay the sum that may deliver me.
Duke: Speak freely, Syracusan, what thou wilt.[3]
Egeon: [*to Antipholus*] Is not your name, sir, called Antipholus?
And is not that your bondman[4] Dromio?

[1] *allow me to*
[2] *possibly, perhaps*
[3] *ask whatever you want*
[4] *servant*

Egeon is dismayed to discover that neither man recognises him. He wonders whether his burden of sorrow has changed his appearance over the years since the two young men left Syracuse:

Egeon: Why look you strange on me? You know me well.
Antipholus of Ephesus: I never saw you in my life till now.
Egeon: O, grief hath changed me since you saw me last,
And careful[1] hours with Time's deformed hand
Have written strange defeatures[2] in my face.
But tell me yet, dost thou not know my voice?
Antipholus of Ephesus: Neither.
Egeon: Dromio, nor thou?
Dromio of Ephesus: No, trust me, sir, nor I.

[1] *anguished, troubled*
[2] *blemishes, wrinkles*

A long time has passed since his son left home, aged eighteen, on his quest for his lost twin; and Egeon himself has, in turn, been on a long, fruitless journey, hoping for news of the errant youth. The years of anxiety must have taken their toll on his voice too, Egeon realises. Nevertheless, he is convinced that the man in front of him is the son he has been searching for:

Egeon: Not know my voice! – O Time's extremity,[1]
Hast thou so cracked and splitted my poor tongue
In seven short years that here my only son
Knows not my feeble key of untuned cares?[2]
… Yet hath my night of life[3] some memory,
My wasting lamps[4] some fading glimmer left,
My dull deaf ears a little use to hear;
All these old witnesses – I cannot err –
Tell me thou art my son Antipholus.

[1] *severity, ruthlessness*
[2] *does not recognise my frail voice, made harsh by my sorrows*
[3] *old age*
[4] *my failing eyes*

Antipholus now makes a revelation that leaves Egeon devastated. Even so, he clings on, desperately, to the possibility that this is his son:

Antipholus of Ephesus: I never saw my father in my life.
Egeon: But seven years since,[1] in Syracusa, boy,
Thou knowst we parted. But perhaps, my son,
Thou sham'st to acknowledge me in misery.[2]
Antipholus of Ephesus: The Duke and all that know me in the city
Can witness with me that it is not so.
I ne'er saw Syracusa in my life.

[1] *only seven years ago*
[2] *you're ashamed to acknowledge me in my miserable state*

The duke confirms that Antipholus has never, to his knowledge, been to Syracuse. He remarks, sadly, that Egeon's tragic situation seems to have affected his sanity:

> *Duke:* I see thy age and dangers make thee dote.[1]
>
> [1] *have caused you to lose your mind*

Together again

The abbess now arrives. With her are the two men who have been sheltering in her abbey, Antipholus and Dromio of Syracuse.

The bystanders are stunned as the new arrivals come face to face with their living images: which is real, and which is the apparition? One of each pair, surely, must have come from beyond this world. The duke looks first and Antipholus and his double, and then turns to the two Dromios:

> *Adriana:* I see two husbands, or mine eyes deceive me.
> *Duke:* One of these men is genius[1] to the other;
> And so of these,[2] which is the natural man
> And which the spirit? Who deciphers them?
>
> [1] *guardian spirit, other-worldly protector*
> [2] *the same is true of the Dromios*

Both Dromios claim to be genuine, and warn the duke that the other is a fraud:

> *Dromio of Syracuse:* I, sir, am Dromio; command him away.
> *Dromio of Ephesus:* I, sir, am Dromio; pray, let me stay.

The newly-arrived pair then notice an elderly man, tied up in preparation for his execution. They recognise him at once:

> *Antipholus of Syracuse:* Egeon, art thou not? Or else his ghost.
> *Dromio of Syracuse:* O my old master! – Who hath bound him here?

Another astonishing revelation now occurs. The abbess too can identify the condemned man, and she steps forward to free him from the ropes in which he is bound:

Abbess: Whoever bound him, I will loose his bonds,
And gain a husband by his liberty. [*Unbinds him.*]
Speak, old Egeon, if the be'st the man
That hadst a wife once called Emilia,
That bore thee at a burden[1] two fair sons.
O, if thou be'st the same Egeon, speak,
And speak unto the same Emilia.

[1] *in a single birth*

Emilia, the abbess, reveals that, like Egeon, she was rescued from the shipwreck with two baby boys, one her own and one adopted. However, the boys were stolen from her by fishermen from Corinth, and she never saw them again. She herself became a nun, and has spent the long years since their tragic separation in the abbey in Ephesus.

Antipholus and Dromio confirm excitedly that they were indeed brought up in Corinth before coming to Ephesus. The family of Emilia and Egeon, it seems, is finally reunited.

> "... the reconciliation scene ends a truly important human crisis, as well as resolving the comic confusions of the central tale. Shakespeare, even as a young man at the beginning of his career, felt that a happy ending should not be divorced from an awareness of mortality and human frailty. In this he utterly transcends the genre of farce."
>
>   Charles Boyce, *Shakespeare A to Z*, 1990

But the confusion is not yet over. Adriana wants to establish the truth about the day's perplexing events and her husband's strange behaviour. As the identities of the twin brothers become clear, it emerges that Adriana's sister may also have found a husband:

> *Adriana:* Which of you two did dine with me today?
> *Antipholus of Syracuse:* I, gentle mistress.
> *Adriana:* [*to Antipholus of Syracuse*] And are not you my husband?
> *Antipholus of Ephesus:* No, I say nay to that.
> *Antipholus of Syracuse:* And so do I, yet[1] did she call me so;
> And this fair gentlewoman, her sister here,
> Did call me brother. [*to Luciana*] What I told you then
> I hope I shall have leisure to make good,
> If this be not a dream I see and hear.
>
> [1] *even though*

Angelo notices that Antipholus of Syracuse is wearing the gold chain requested by his brother. The fact that he gave the chain to the wrong Antipholus, Angelo realises, led to quarrelling, an arrest and a near duel; but any hard feelings, they all agree, are now forgotten.

Adriana remembers another puzzling episode. On hearing of her husband's arrest, she had given Dromio a purse full of gold coins to pay his bail. As far as she knows, the money never arrived. Again, it becomes clear that the money went to the wrong Antipholus.

The purse is now returned to Adriana's husband, who immediately offers it to the duke, to pay Egeon's ransom and save his life. There is no need, the duke assures him. Gladly putting aside his earlier inflexibility, he declares that Egeon is now a free man:

> *Adriana:* I sent you money, sir, to be your bail,
> By Dromio, but I think he brought it not.
> *Dromio of Ephesus:* No, none by me.
> *Antipholus of Syracuse:* This purse of ducats I received from you,
> And Dromio my man did bring them me ...
> [*Gives his brother the purse.*]

Antipholus of Ephesus: These ducats pawn I for my father here.[1]
Duke: It shall not need: thy father hath his life.

> [1] *I am offering this money as payment for my father's release*

The courtesan now steps forward; one final error needs to be put right. With no prospect of receiving her promised gold chain, she must content herself with the return of her property:

Courtesan: Sir, I must have that diamond[1] from you.
Antipholus of Ephesus: [*Gives her the ring.*] There, take it, and much thanks for my good cheer.[2]

> [1] *diamond ring*
> [2] *your pleasant company*

New beginnings

The abbess invites everyone to come into the abbey to talk about the day's complicated, tangled events. She is confident that anyone upset during the confusion of the past few hours can be comforted, and that harmony can be restored:

Abbess: ... all that are assembled in this place,
That by this sympathized one day's error
Have suffered wrong,[1] go, keep us company,
And we shall make full satisfaction.[2]

> [1] *who have suffered though the strange series of related errors that have taken place today*
> [2] *amends*

"Witches, fiends and sorcerers ... all evaporate when the Abbess appears. Even the Duke's harsh justice is tempered with Christian charity; the devil is truly exorcised."

Ellen Goodman, RSC programme notes for the 1983 production of *The Comedy of Errors*

Emilia has waited many years for this reunion with her family, and is longing to learn more about her husband and her sons. After all these years, she feels as if she is meeting them for the first time. The duke is eager to join the celebrations:

Abbess: The Duke, my husband, and my children both,
And you, the calendars of their nativity,[1]
Go to a gossips' feast,[2] and joy[3] with me.
After so long grief, such felicity!
Duke: With all my heart I'll gossip at this feast.

[1] *the two Dromios, born on exactly the same day as Emilia's twins*
[2] *celebration of a birth or baptism*
[3] *rejoice*

The people gathered in the marketplace now drift away: the reunited parents, the duke and his attendants, Angelo, the merchant, Adriana and Luciana, and the courtesan all make their way to the abbey.

There is a final, brief moment of confusion as Dromio asks about the ship waiting in the harbour. He has moved his master's goods from the Centaur inn, as instructed, and loaded them on board ship. Now that the two of them are staying in Ephesus, the goods can be unloaded again. Not for the first time, Dromio chooses the wrong Antipholus:

Dromio of Syracuse: Master, shall I fetch your stuff from shipboard?
Antipholus of Ephesus: Dromio, what stuff of mine hast thou
   embarked?
Dromio of Syracuse: Your goods that lay at host,[1] sir, in the Centaur.
Antipholus of Syracuse: He speaks to me; – I am your master,
   Dromio.
   Come, go with us; we'll look to that anon.[2]

[1] *that were stored at the inn*
[2] *we'll deal with that soon*

The Antipholus brothers join the others in the abbey, leaving the two Dromios alone in the marketplace.

> *"These two long-suffering clowns have had to sustain numerous blows from the Antipholuses throughout the play, and the audience is heartened to see them go out in such high good humour ... it remains touching that Shakespeare, from the start, prefers his clowns to his merchants."*
>
> Harold Bloom, *Shakespeare: The Invention of the Human*, 1998

The newly-arrived Dromio touches on the fact that the formidable Nell, the kitchen maid, claimed earlier today to be his wife. That error, thankfully, has been resolved, and from now on she will be his sister-in-law:

Dromio of Syracuse: There is a fat friend at your master's house,
        That kitchened me for you[1] today at dinner;
        She now shall be my sister, not my wife.

   [1] *who invited me into her kitchen, mistaking me for you*

The two of them decide to make their way to the abbey. Dromio of Syracuse asks his brother to go first; although they are twins, Dromio of Ephesus is the older, by a matter of minutes. Shrugging off the difference, the two of them link arms and set off side by side:

Dromio of Ephesus: [*embracing his brother*] ... we came into the
        world like brother and brother;
        And now let's go hand in hand, not one before another.

Acknowledgements

The following publications have proved invaluable as sources of factual information and critical insight:

- Catharine Arnold, *Globe: Life in Shakespeare's London*, Simon & Schuster, 2015

- Jonathan Bate, Introduction to the RSC Shakespeare edition of *The Comedy of Errors*, Macmillan, 2011

- Jonathan Bate, *Soul of the Age*, Penguin, 2009

- Harold Bloom, *Shakespeare: The Invention of the Human*, Harper Collins, 1998

- Charles Boyce, *Shakespeare A to Z*, Roundtable Press, 1990

- Ivor Brown, *Shakespeare*, Collins, 1949

- Kent Cartwright, Introduction to the Arden Shakespeare edition of *The Comedy of Errors*, Bloomsbury Publishing, 2016

- Northrop Frye, *Anatomy of Criticism*, Princeton University Press, 1957

- Ellen Goodman, programme notes for *The Comedy of Errors*, Royal Shakespeare Theatre, 1983

- Alexander Leggatt, *Shakespeare's Comedy of Love*, Methuen, 1974

- Laurie Maguire and Emma Smith, *30 Great Myths About Shakespeare*, Wiley-Blackwell, 2013

- Walter Raleigh, *Shakespeare*, Macmillan, 1957

- Gamini Salgado, *Time's Deformed Hand*, in *Shakespeare Survey 25*, Cambridge University Press, 1972

- Charles Whitworth, Introduction to the Oxford Shakespeare edition of *The Comedy of Errors*, Oxford University Press, 2002

- Michael Wood, *In Search of Shakespeare*, BBC Books, 2005

Guides currently available in the *Shakespeare Handbooks* series are:

- **Antony & Cleopatra** (ISBN 978 1 899747 02 3, £4.95)
- **As You Like It** (ISBN 978 1 899747 00 9, £4.95)
- **The Comedy of Errors** (ISBN 978 1 899747 16 0, £4.95)
- **Hamlet** (ISBN 978 1 899747 07 8, £4.95)
- **Henry IV, Part 1** (ISBN 978 1 899747 05 4, £4.95)
- **Julius Caesar** (ISBN 978 1 899747 11 5, £4.95)
- **King Lear** (ISBN 978 1 899747 03 0, £4.95)
- **Macbeth** (ISBN 978 1 899747 04 7, £4.95)
- **Measure for Measure** (ISBN 978 1 899747 14 6, £4.95)
- **The Merchant of Venice** (ISBN 978 1 899747 13 9, £4.95)
- **A Midsummer Night's Dream** (ISBN 978 1 899747 09 2, £4.95)
- **Othello** (ISBN 978 1 899747 12 2, £4.95)
- **Romeo & Juliet** (ISBN 978 1 899747 10 8, £4.95)
- **The Tempest** (ISBN 978 1 899747 08 5, £4.95)
- **Twelfth Night** (ISBN 978 1 899747 01 6, £4.95)
- **The Winter's Tale** (ISBN 978 1 899747 15 3, £4.95)

www.shakespeare-handbooks.com

Details correct at time of going to press. Whilst every effort is made to keep prices low, Upstart Crow Publications reserves the right to show new retail prices on covers which may differ from those previously advertised in the text or elsewhere.